es
he
on

STORYLAND
CROSS STITCH

What Delilah Did
~PRESENTS~

STORYLAND
CROSS STITCH

COLLINS & BROWN

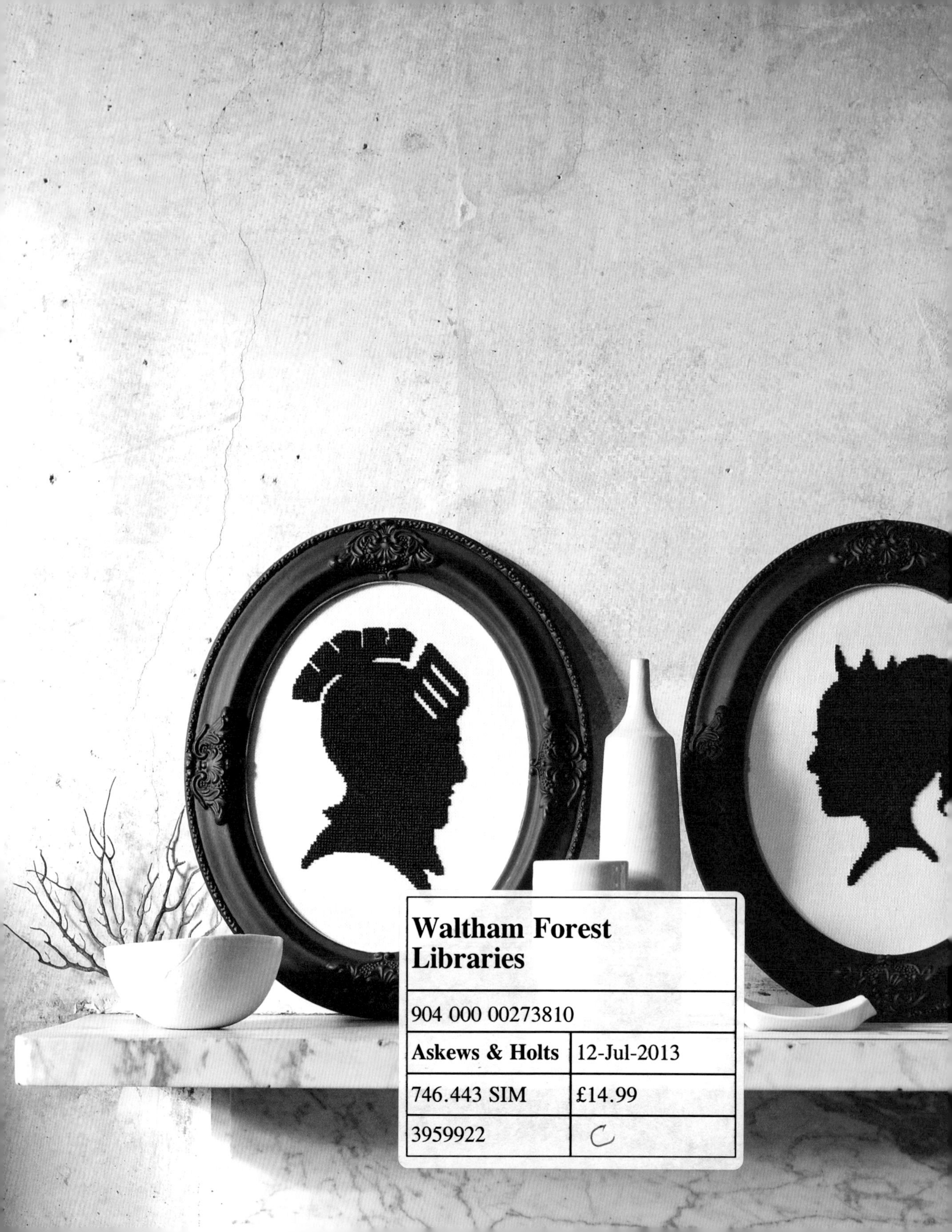

Contents

Hello there!

I feel I must begin with a warning to all who wander here:
you will find no fluffy kittens in the patterns within these pages;
no teddy bears carrying declarations of love. It is not that kind
of book... Here be beauties and beasties from long, long ago;
from nature and magic and stories of old.

If you want to spark your imagination and whisk your thoughts
off to far-away locations, then you have come to the right place.
I have created a collection of things that, I hope you will
agree, are as lovely to make as they are to behold.

The projects in this book are really just meant as a starting point –
patterns and ideas to be mixed and jumbled together to your
heart's desire. You can stitch the key onto a pencil case, or
the jackalope onto a cushion. I will even consent to your
stitching the patterns in baby pink if you feel you must!

If you are new to cross stitch, never fear, it is as
easy as pie. Turn the page and I will explain all.

Delilah

x

Equipment & Materials

{1. YOU WILL NEED}

Embroidery fabric: linen, evenweave or aida

Embroidery thread

Tapestry needle(s)

Small, sharp scissors

Pattern sheet

A pen or pencil

A comfy place to sit

Good lighting

… and patience!

{2. OPTIONAL EXTRAS}

Hoops and frames

Using a hoop or a frame when you are stitching is not a prerequisite, though I find it makes cross stitch a lot easier and helps to keep the stitches looking neat.

Hoops and frames that accommodate the entire design in one go – rather than moving a smaller hoop from place to place – are far preferable, as the latter can distort the stitches, but this is entirely a matter of personal preference.

Just remember that hoops are measured by their maximum diameter, so if you are looking for a hoop to house a pattern that measures 18 x 18cm (7 x 7in), the chances are it will not fit into an 18cm (7in) hoop!

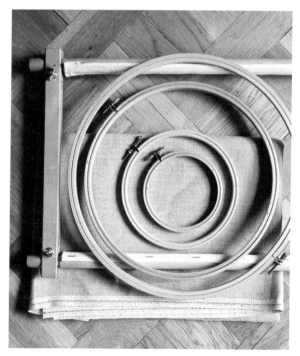

Fabric

Counted cross stitch is most commonly worked on evenweave linen or aida cloth. These fabrics are woven with the same number of threads per inch in the warp and weft, meaning that the holes between the woven threads form a grid of squares (like graph paper) that correspond to the pattern you are following.

Aida is woven in blocks that create very obvious squares to work on, making it perfect for beginners, whereas stitching over two threads at a time forms the squares on evenweave or linen. Stitching on linen or evenweave takes a little more thought, but the finish is far nicer.

Evenweave fabrics come in different 'thread counts'. The higher the count, the finer the fabric and the smaller your stitches (and the finished design) will be. Linen is counted by the number of individual threads per inch and aida is counted by the number of blocks per inch, so stitches worked on a 14-count aida will be the same size as those worked on a 28-count linen, because the linen is worked over two threads at a time.

If you are new to counted cross stitch, a good fabric to start with is 14-count aida or 28-count linen, as the stitches are large enough to count easily while you get the hang of things. The patterns in this book state the size of the finished design when it is stitched on a particular fabric, so if you prefer to use fabric with a lower thread count be sure to allow extra fabric. Correspondingly, less fabric will be needed for a higher thread count.

Needles

The best needles to use for cross stitch are blunt tapestry needles. The rounded end means that the needle passes only through the ready-made gaps between the threads rather than piercing threads or blocks in the fabric, and this keeps your stitches nice and neat.

I find that size 24 or 26 needles work well for the most commonly used fabrics.

Thread

The most frequently used thread for counted cross stitch is stranded cotton. Threads are loosely twisted together so that their six strands can be easily split for stitching with different thicknesses, depending on the weight of your fabric and the size of the stitches. The thickness of the thread is mainly a question of personal preference.

Each pattern in this book suggests the best number of strands to use, but feel free to increase or reduce the number of strands, as you wish, for your own stitching.

The table below is a guide to the number of strands I use for different fabrics.

Number of Strands	Aida	Linen
3 or 4	14-count	28-count
2 or 3	16-count	32-count
2 or 3	18-count	36-count
2	20-count	40-count

MEASURING TAPE

PENCIL

EMBROIDERY THREADS AND FABRICS

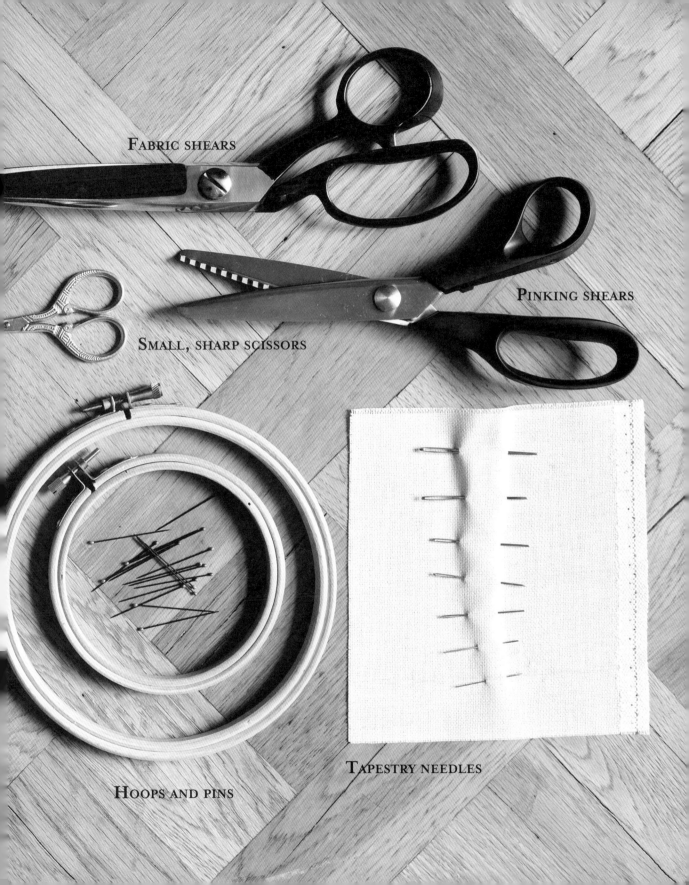

FABRIC SHEARS

PINKING SHEARS

SMALL, SHARP SCISSORS

TAPESTRY NEEDLES

HOOPS AND PINS

Cross stitch, also known as counted cross stitch, is a simple, universal stitch that can be picked up really quickly. So it's ideal for beginners, but depending on the scale and complexity of the design, it can also create quite challenging patterns that will stretch the skills of those with considerable experience. The basic techniques outlined here will stand you in good stead whatever level you want to attain.

{1. PREPARING THE FABRIC}

Embroidery fabric is woven so that its threads form a grid of squares to work over, which correspond to the grid on the cross stitch pattern sheet. Most of the designs in this book are stitched onto evenweave or linen fabric, which means that each stitch is worked over two threads rather than one. This means that you need to imagine that the grid of squares is formed over two threads at a time in each direction (see below).

For aida fabric or waste canvas, each square will be formed over one block at a time instead of two, as shown above.

It is always best to iron your fabric before you begin because stubborn creases are much more difficult to remove once you have stitched over them. Once your fabric is smooth, you need to find its centre so that you know where to position the pattern. To do this, fold the fabric in half one way, open it out again, and then fold it in half the other way, gently pressing along the middle of each fold to find the point where they cross. Once you have found the centre point, mark it with a pin or your needle until you are ready to begin stitching.

{2. USING A HOOP OR FRAME}

If you are using a hoop, loosen the screw at the top of the hoop and take apart the two rings. Place the inner ring on a flat surface and lay the fabric, centred, on top of it. Place the outer ring on top of the fabric, and push it down to sandwich the fabric between the two rings. Tighten the screw, making sure the fabric is held taut in the hoop.

For larger designs you may wish to use a roller frame. In this case, choose a frame that has rollers long enough to accommodate at least the shortest side of your fabric – you can then wind the length around the bars and roll the fabric up and down as necessary to complete your design.

Clip or sew (with a loose running stitch) one side of your fabric to the first roller bar, and then fix the opposite side of the fabric to the second roller bar in the same way. Once both sides are secure, loosen the screws on either side of each roller and wind the fabric around the rollers until you can see the centre point that you marked previously.

Once you have the fabric where you want it, tighten the screws on one of the roller bars, wind the other bar a little tighter until the fabric is taut, and then tighten the screws on the second bar too. The fabric is then ready for stitching.

{3. PREPARING THE THREAD}

Cut a length of thread about as long as your arm. The thread is made up of six strands, and these need to be separated before use. To do this, find the end of one strand and hold it firmly between your thumb and forefinger. With your other hand, loosely hold the rest of the strands together and gently push them down while you pull the single strand up and out of the thread.

Straighten out the remaining strands and repeat until you are left with six separate strands. Now take the required number of separated strands (see page II) and line them up together to form one thread that is the right number of strands thick. The thread is now ready to stitch with.

{4. FINDING THE STARTING POINT}

Cross stitch is worked in rows of stitches and each dot in the pattern represents a complete cross stitch.

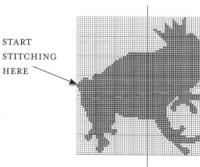

START
STITCHING
HERE →

To find the point to start stitching, first locate the centre point of the pattern, as shown above. Then count the number of stitches back to the start of the middle row. If you are working over two threads at a time onto evenweave or linen, double this number and count that many holes to the left from the centre of the fabric.

{5. BEGINNING TO STITCH}

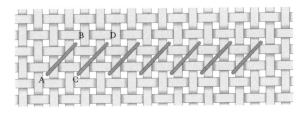

Rather than knotting the thread at the back of the fabric to secure it, instead leave 5–10cm (2–4in) of loose end to tidy up later, as this is far neater.

Come up through the fabric at your starting point (A) and make the first diagonal 'half-stitch' by inserting the needle back through the fabric at point B. Pull the needle back up through the fabric at point C and down again through point D. Continue in this way to the end of the row (see above), counting the number of stitches from the pattern.

When you get to the end of the row (or a gap in continuous stitches), go back and 'cross' the stitches you have just made. This time you need to work from right to left: come up through the fabric at E, insert the needle back through the surface at F, come up again through G and back down through H (see above).

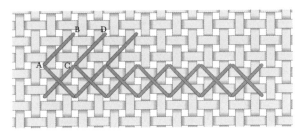

The back of the fabric at this point should look like the stitching details shown above.

Once all of the cross stitches in this row or section are complete, move onto the row above, or onto another section, marking off each row of the pattern as you go so that you do not lose your place.

If the next row up would normally begin with a stitch at the same point as the previous cross stitch ended (point A), reverse the next half-stitch by working it from B to A (see above). Continue the row by stitching from C to D as normal.

Knotless Loop Start

If you are working with an even number of strands – for example, two or four – you can save time when beginning a new thread by using a knotless loop instead of leaving a loose end to tidy up later.

To do this, you need to prepare the thread slightly differently to the normal routine. For example, to stitch with four strands using this method, take two long strands of thread, line them up together as usual and then fold the length in half so that you have a single length of thread that is four strands thick with four loose strands at one end and a loop at the other.

Thread the end with the loose strands through the eye of the needle. When you have done this, bring the needle up through the underside of the fabric where you wish to begin stitching, leaving a few centimetres of thread (the end with the loop) underneath.

Put the needle back through the surface of the fabric to form your first stitch, and then through the middle of the loop that has been left at the back (see above). Once the thread is pulled all the way through the loop it will be fixed to the fabric – with no need for a knot.

{6. COMING TO THE END OF THE THREAD}

When you only have 10cm (4in) or so of thread left, run the needle underneath four or five completed stitches on the back of the fabric to secure it without a knot, then neatly snip off the loose end (see below). Tidy any loose ends left from when you started stitching in the same way.

Loose end threaded underneath completed stitches.

The back of your fabric should look almost as neat as the front. If you come to a gap or a jump in a sequence of stitches, it is generally better to finish the thread you are working on and start afresh in the next section than to carry the thread behind large expanses of fabric, as it could show through (especially when using black thread on light fabric). Alternatively, you can fasten the thread behind existing stitches over short distances, as if you were finishing a thread off. However, be careful not to pull stitches out of shape when doing this.

{7. FLIP IT}

Once you have completed all of the rows and sections in the top half of the pattern, turn the hoop and the pattern upside down. Now stitch the bottom half of the design from the centre to the base, marking off each row as you go, just as you have done before.

Always make sure that you work all of your stitches in the same direction to keep the finished embroidery looking uniform. Turning the hoop upside down (180 degrees) will not change the direction of your stitches if you work them all in the same order (for example, A-B-C-D as in the diagrams). However, turning the hoop to the side (90 or 270 degrees) will mean the stitches face a different way.

{8. FINISHING OFF}

When you have finished your pattern you will need to remove any creases before you can display it. To do this, place it face down on a folded towel to protect the stitches and dampen the back with a light mist of water. Carefully iron the back of the fabric with a medium iron until the creases are gone. It is then ready to use.

{TIPS}

{AFTER ABOUT EVERY 10 STITCHES, LET THE NEEDLE 'DROP' AND SPIN TO ALLOW THE THREAD TO UNWIND ITSELF. THE SHORTER THE THREAD BECOMES, THE MORE OFTEN YOU WILL NEED TO DO THIS TO MAKE SURE THE THREAD DOES NOT TWIST AROUND ITSELF TOO MUCH AND BEGIN TO KNOT.}

{IF YOU ARE USING A HOOP TO STRETCH THE FABRIC, REMOVE YOUR EMBROIDERY FROM THE HOOP WHEN YOU ARE NOT STITCHING SO THAT IT WON'T MARK THE FABRIC.}

{KEEP THE TENSION OF YOUR THREAD AND STITCHES QUITE LOOSE AT ALL TIMES, AND WHEN PULLING THE THREAD THROUGH THE FABRIC FOR EACH STITCH, STOP AS SOON AS THERE IS RESISTANCE. IF YOU PULL THE STITCHES TOO TIGHT THIS WILL SHOW UP GAPS OF FABRIC BETWEEN THE STITCHES AND MAKE IT VERY DIFFICULT TO RUN THREADS UNDERNEATH COMPLETED STITCHES AT THE BACK OF YOUR WORK.}

{projects for beginners}

The Secret Key

T IS FAIR TO SAY that I am a curious sort of a person, and if you have ever met one of my kind you will know that curiosity is an incurable condition. Which explains why, when I came across an abandoned cottage at the end of an overgrown track, there was simply no way that I was going to leave well enough alone.

Nestled on top of the crooked old doorframe, amongst the spiders and the dust, you will find a secret key. It is a small, rather grubby golden affair with a head shaped a little like a squashed heart: the exact same squashed heart that is etched into the metal below the keyhole.

The key turns.
The lock clicks.
The door swings open.

This is no ordinary cottage.

This is Storyland...

Secret Key Bookmark

{SUPPLIES}

27-count ivory evenweave fabric,
6 x 15cm (2⅜ x 6in) – 28-count
fabric would also work for
this design

Metallic gold thread (Kreinik
Fine Braid #8), 4m (13ft)

Tapestry needle, size 24 or 26

Sharp embroidery needle

Small, sharp scissors

Natural calico fabric, 8 x 17cm
(3⅛ x 6¾in)

1.

Cut the evenweave fabric to 6 x 15cm
(2⅜ x 6in). Because the edges will be
on show it is important to cut neatly
along a straight line between two
individual threads, as shown below.
Following these threads will ensure
that all of your edges end up straight.

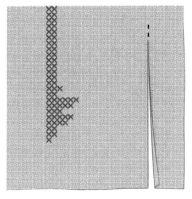

STEP 1

2.

Follow the instructions on pages 14–15
to prepare your evenweave fabric, find
its centre point and prepare a length
of thread – if you are using Kreinik
Fine Braid #8 you will need to stitch
the design using a single strand.

3.

Working from the centre point
outwards, follow the pattern on
the opposite page to stitch the key.

4.

When you have finished stitching,
carefully handwash the fabric, if
necessary, and iron it face down
over a towel; this will act as a cushion
to protect your stitches.

5.

Fray each edge of the evenweave
fabric by gently pulling away a couple
of threads (see below). You may find
that some threads came away while
you were stitching, in which case you
simply need to even up the other
edges by removing the same number
of threads from each.

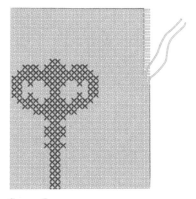

STEP 5

{SECRET KEY PATTERN}

6.

If you've not already done so, cut the calico fabric to 8 x 17cm (3⅛ x 6¾in), again trying to cut in as straight a line between the threads in the weave as possible. (Alternatively, a rather nifty characteristic of calico is that you can cut a notch at the edge of the fabric and rip it apart – it will automatically rip in a straight line!) Fray the edges by pulling a number of threads from each side until they look even.

7.

Align the two pieces of fabric so that the calico is backing your embroidery, pin them together and sew neatly around the edge of the evenweave with a running stitch using the sharp embroidery needle with more of the gold thread. You can follow the lines in the evenweave fabric – three threads in from the edge is about right – and count holes to help keep your stitches an even length.

8.

Secure the ends by making a couple of backstitches, threading the loose end between the two layers of fabric and cutting off the excess.

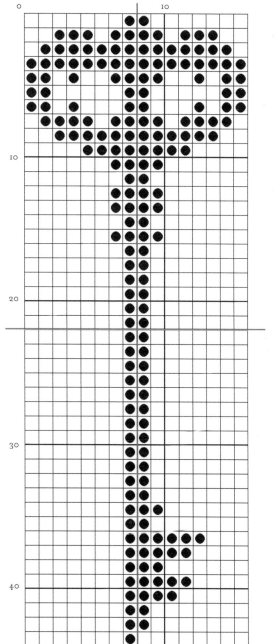

Centre Points

16 x 44 stitches

Total stitches: 187

Kreinik Fine Braid #8,
Shade 002 Gold

- - -

187 stitches @ 1 strand
= 4m/13ft (½ reel)

Design size on 27-count
evenweave: 3.2 x 8.5cm
(1¼ x 3⅜in)

Approx stitching time: 1¼ hours

Fantabulous Mr Fox

Y FRIEND ALICE once told me that arriving in an entirely new world with not the slightest inkling of what you might find there can be a very daunting prospect. What you really need is a guide; someone who knows the lay of the land and can help you on your way.

On that note, allow me to introduce you to Mr Fox.

You can probably tell from his mischievous gaze and dashing good looks that he has rather a high opinion of himself, but I am inclined to forgive him because he is FANTABULOUS.

I am fully aware that this may be a controversial statement to make (especially if you have ever owned hens), but there is not a soul in the land who can rival Mr Fox for intelligence, cunning and sheer nerve. If you want something doing, Mr Fox is your man – or, more accurately, your vulpine.

With little more than a swish of his ginger tail he can achieve the seemingly impossible, so it may be wise to keep him close – if you ever find yourself abandoned in Storyland, you will want him on your side.

Bow & Arrow Needle Book

{SUPPLIES}

32-count linen, 20 x 15cm
(8 x 6in)

Stranded cotton embroidery
thread in Duck Egg (Anchor
No. 975/DMC No. 828) and
Cream (Anchor No. 926/
DMC No. 712), 2 strands

Tapestry needle, size 26 or 28

Sharp sewing needle

Small, sharp scissors

Natural calico fabric or similar
cotton fabric, 20 x 15cm
(8 x 6in)

Sewing machine or needle and
sewing thread (to match linen)

Three pieces of wool felt,
12 x 17cm (4¾ x 6¾in) each

I.

Cut the piece of evenweave fabric to
20 x 15cm (8 x 6in) and iron flat.
Fold the fabric halfway along the
longest side to form the two covers
of your book (each 10 x 15cm/4 x 6in).
To find the place to start stitching
the front cover, fold the fabric back
to meet the spine and press the
centre point.

STEP 1

2.

Open out again, then fold the whole
cover in half the other way (your
original fabric is now folded into
quarters) and press the centre point
in that direction too. Re-open and
mark the point where the two folds
cross in the centre of the front cover
with a pin or needle.

STEP 2

3.

Follow the instructions on page 15 to prepare a length of thread – this design is stitched with two strands. You can use an embroidery hoop to hold the fabric if you find it helpful, but this is not essential.

4.

Working from the centre point outwards, follow the pattern on page 40 to stitch the bow and arrow on the front cover.

5.

Repeat steps 1 to 3 and follow the pattern on page 41 to stitch the quiver of arrows on the back cover.

6.

When you have finished stitching both covers, carefully handwash the fabric, if necessary, and iron it face down over a towel; this will act as a cushion to protect your stitches.

7.

Cut a piece of calico or cotton lining fabric to 20 x 15cm (8 x 6in). Pin the embroidered linen and lining fabric together, right sides together.

8.

Using a sewing machine or needle and thread, sew the two pieces of fabric together about 0.5cm (¼in) from the edge, leaving a 4–5cm (1½–2in) gap on one of the edges for turning right side out later. Secure the end of the thread with a couple of backstitches. Snip off the four corners, making sure not to cut into the seam. Press the seams open with an iron.

STEP 8

9.

Turn the shape out the right way through the open part of the seam. Place the turned-out fabric face down on a towel (to protect the stitches) and iron the shape flat.

10.

Neatly topstitch all the way around the four sides of the cover, just a few millimetres from the edge. This will flatten the seams and also close the edge that was left open from turning right side out. Secure the end of the thread with a couple of backstitches and weave the loose end inside the two pieces of fabric.

11.

Fold the cover in half and press the fold with an iron, taking care to avoid passing the iron over the embroidered stitches as this will flatten them.

12.

Cut three pieces of felt to 12 x 17cm (4¾ x 6¾in), and fold each piece in half along its longest side to form two pages (each 8.5 x 12cm/3⅜ x 4¾in), and then iron each one flat along the fold.

13.

Open out all three of the felt pages and layer them on top of the open cover, lining up the spines.

14.

Pin the felt pages to the cover and sew all the way along the spine with a small, neat running stitch through all four layers (see below). Secure the end of the thread with a couple of backstitches and weave the loose thread end inside the two pieces of fabric.

STEP 14

(THE FELT FOR THIS PROJECT IS QUITE THICK – AROUND 1MM (¹⁄₁₆IN) PER SHEET. IF YOU ARE USING THINNER FELT YOU CAN AFFORD TO ADD A COUPLE OF EXTRA PAGES TO YOUR NEEDLE BOOK TO END UP WITH THE SAME OVERALL THICKNESS OF PAGES. YOU SHOULD CUT, LAYER AND SEW THEM TOGETHER IN EXACTLY THE SAME WAY.)

Golden Goose Lavender Sachet

{SUPPLIES}

32-count dark linen, 20 x 20cm (8 x 8in)

Metallic gold thread (Kreinik Fine Braid #8), 7m (23ft)

Tapestry needle, size 26 or 28

Sharp embroidery needle

Small, sharp scissors

Natural calico fabric or similar cotton fabric, 20 x 20cm (8 x 8in)

Sewing machine or needle and sewing thread (to match linen)

Dried lavender

1.
Cut the piece of evenweave fabric to 20 x 20cm (8 x 8in). Follow the instructions on pages 14–15 to prepare your evenweave fabric, find its centre point and prepare a length of thread – if you are using Kreinik Fine Braid #8, you will need to stitch the design using a single strand. You can use a hoop to hold the fabric while you stitch if you find it helpful, but it is not essential.

2.
Working from the centre point outwards, follow the pattern on page 47 to stitch the goose.

3.
When you have finished stitching, carefully handwash the fabric, if necessary, and iron it face down over a towel; this will act as a cushion to protect your stitches.

4.
Cut a piece of calico or similar cotton fabric to 20 x 20cm (8 x 8in) and place your embroidery face down on top of it. Pin the two pieces of fabric together, right sides in.

5.
Using a sewing machine or needle and thread, sew the two pieces of fabric together about 1cm (⅜in) from the edge, leaving a 4–5cm (1½–2in) gap on one of the edges for turning right side out later. Secure the end of the thread with a couple of backstitches.

6.
Snip off the four corners, making sure not to cut into the seam, and press the seams open with an iron.

7.
Turn the shape right side out through the opening in the seam, place the turned-out sachet face down on a towel (to protect the stitches) and iron the sachet flat.

{IF YOU ARE NOT KEEN ON THE SCENT OF LAVENDER, YOU CAN SUBSTITUTE OTHER DRIED FILLINGS SUCH AS ROSEBUDS OR CHAMOMILE FLOWERS. ANOTHER ALTERNATIVE IS TO COMBINE A FEW CLOVES OR SLICED CINNAMON STICKS WITH SOME NATURAL GRAINS FOR A SPICY SCENT CONSIDER ADDING EXTRA LINING TO YOUR SACHET IF YOU OPT FOR THESE.}

8.

Neatly topstitch about 3cm (1⅛in)
from the edge around all four sides of
the sachet, stopping about 5cm (2in)
short of closing the last edge.

9.

Without removing the sachet from the
machine (or needle and thread if you
are stitching by hand), spoon the dried
lavender into the middle section of
the sachet – five tablespoons should be
enough, but add as much as you wish.

10.

Pin the remaining open edge
together (if you don't pin it, the bulk
of the lavender will pull the edges
out of line) and continue sewing
along the edge to close the gap and
hold the lavender in the centre of the
sachet. Secure the thread with a
couple of backstitches.

11.

Neatly topstitch around the very edge
of the sachet. This will flatten the
seams and also close the edge that was
left open from turning right side out.

12.

Secure the end of the thread with a
couple of backstitches and weave the
loose thread end inside the two pieces
of fabric.

13.

If you wish, you can add a decorative
running stitch around the centre
panel of the sachet. To do this, use
a sharp embroidery needle to sew a
neat running stitch over the top of
the existing topstitch line. Once you
have stitched around all four sides,
secure the thread with a couple of
backstitches, take the needle and
thread in between the two layers of
fabric, then back out of the fabric
and trim the excess length.

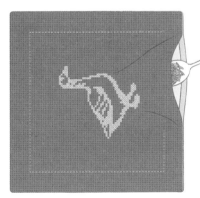

STEP 9

STEP 13

{GOLDEN GOOSE PATTERN}

Approx
stitching
time:
2¾ hours

Centre Points

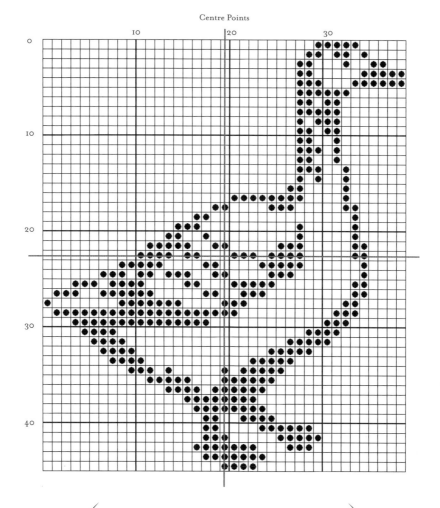

39 x 45 stitches

Total stitches: 368

Design size on 32-count linen:
6.2 x 7.1cm (2½ x 2¾in)

Thread: Kreinik Fine Braid #8,
colour 002 Gold, 1 strand
= 7m/23ft (²⁄₃ reel)

Life in Miniature

S A GENERAL RULE, we humans tend to walk around with our eyes almost closed, seeing only the obvious and blinkered to everything else. It is all too easy to forget that beneath our feet and over our heads live insects and invertebrates, birds and bees, and, in the case of Storyland, an entire fairy world.

The fairies keep to themselves. A few of them make the crossover, mostly lured by the promise of fame and influence over Storyland's more powerful inhabitants, but in all honesty there isn't much their magic can't provide – they have their own king, their own hierarchy, an entirely separate life in miniature. Why, then, would they want to get mixed up with the rest of us?

More often than not it is we outsiders who seek out fairies in the hope of finding a magical quick fix to our troubles – and as Gertie the Golden Goose will tell you, we have a knack of wishing for the very thing that will be our ruin. It is entirely understandable therefore that the fairy people make it their business to stay hidden.

Wouldn't you?

Miniature Motifs: Embroidered Buttons

{SUPPLIES}

Assorted scraps of 32-count linen or evenweave fabric, minimum size 7 x 7cm (2¾ x 2¾in) each

Stranded cotton thread in assorted colours in Mocha (Anchor No. 393/ DMC No. 3790), Eau de Nil (Anchor No. 847/DMC No. 3072), Dusty Grape (Anchor No. 872/DMC No. 3740), Shadow (Anchor No. 232/DMC No. 452) and Cream (Anchor No. 926/DMC No. 712) – 1m (3ft) per button

Tapestry needle, size 26 or 28

Small, sharp scissors

Self-cover button blanks, 29mm (1⅛in) and 38mm (1½in) diameters

Pencil

Scissors for cutting paper or card

Sewing thread for finishing buttons

I.

Follow the instructions on page 14–15 to prepare a piece of linen and a length of thread for the first button design – you will need a thread thickness of two strands to stitch each pattern. You can use a small 7.5 or 10cm (3 or 4in) hoop to hold the fabric while you stitch if you find it helpful, but this is not essential. If you are using a hoop, remember to cut the fabric large enough for the hoop to hold it; if not, then any scrap fabric that is larger than 7 x 7cm (2¾ x 2¾in) will do the trick.

2.

Follow one of the patterns on pages 54–55 to stitch your chosen design, working from the centre point outwards. The corresponding button size is stated next to each design.

3.

When you have finished stitching, if necessary, iron the fabric as shown on page 18, so that it is then ready for making up.

4.

Cut out the circular template on the back of the button packaging that corresponds to the size of button you are making. Now cut a hole in the middle of the template so that you can see your design through the middle (see below) – this will help you to position your embroidery in the centre of the button.

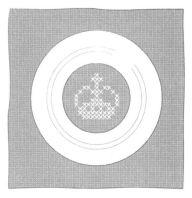

STEP 4

{INCLUDED WITHIN MANY OF THE LARGER PATTERNS THROUGHOUT THE BOOK YOU WILL FIND MORE MINIATURE MOTIFS THAT CAN BE TURNED INTO BUTTONS. IF YOU ARE LUCKY ENOUGH TO HAVE ACCESS TO A BADGE MACHINE, THESE TINY DESIGNS ALSO MAKE PERFECT BADGES AND MAGNETS.}

5.

Position your embroidery in the middle of the circle, mark around the template with a pencil, then cut around the line.

6.

Sew a loose running stitch around the outside of the circle with sewing thread, leaving the end unsecured. Place the circle of embroidered fabric face down, and then put the top half of the blank button (also upside down) on top of the fabric (see below).

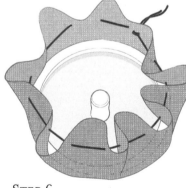

STEP 6

7.

Pull the loose end of the sewing thread to gather the fabric around the button blank, until it is smooth and even on the front. You may wish to zigzag a few stitches across the back of the fabric to pull any stubborn bumps or folds taut around the edge of the button. Secure the sewing thread with a knot or a few backstitches (see below).

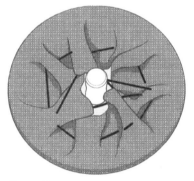

STEP 7

8.

The backing disc to the button blank has a smooth side and a side with teeth. Position the disk with the teeth facing down (towards the fabric) and the hole over the centre post.

9.

Press the disc down hard onto the post, as far as it will go. The teeth on the underside and around the edge of the disc will hold it in place over the fabric. Now your button is ready to sew on to a coat, scarf, bag or a cardigan... or whatever you wish!

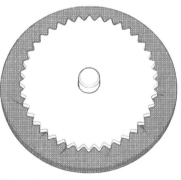

STEP 9

{MINIATURE MOTIFS PATTERNS}

Centre Points

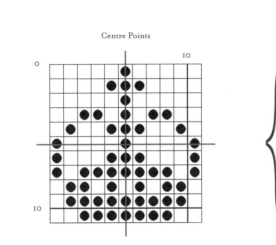

{CROWN}
29mm (1¹⁄₈in) button

11 x 11 stitches

Total stitches: 54

Size on 32-count fabric:
1.7 x 1.7cm (²⁄₃ x ²⁄₃in)

Allow 1m/39in stranded cotton
@ 2 strands

Colour in photo:
Eau de Nil (Anchor No. 847/
DMC No. 3072)

{STAG}
38mm (1½in) button

13 x 15 stitches

Total stitches: 56

Size on 32-count fabric:
2.1 x 2.4cm (³⁄₄ x 1in)

Allow 1m/39in stranded cotton
@ 2 strands

Colour in photo:
Cream (Anchor No. 926/
DMC No. 712)

Centre Points

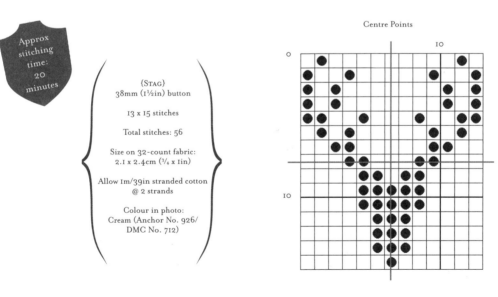

{MINIATURE MOTIFS PATTERNS}

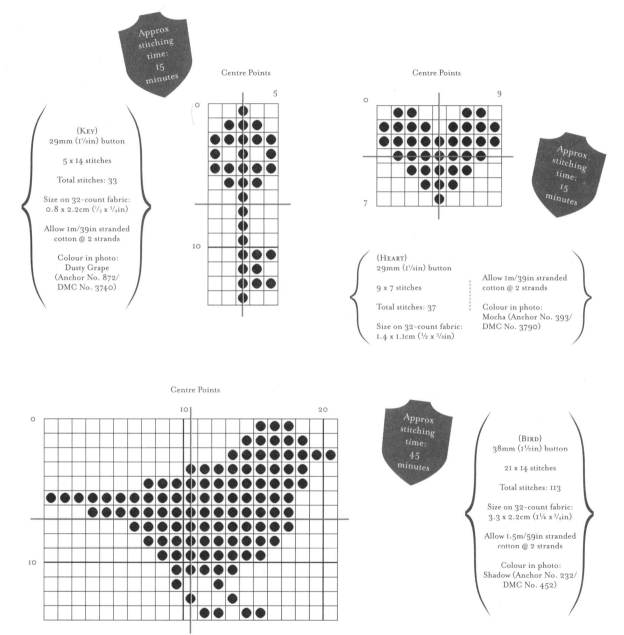

Approx stitching time: 15 minutes

Centre Points

{KEY}
29mm (1⅛in) button

5 x 14 stitches

Total stitches: 33

Size on 32-count fabric:
0.8 x 2.2cm (⅓ x ¾in)

Allow 1m/39in stranded
cotton @ 2 strands

Colour in photo:
Dusty Grape
(Anchor No. 872/
DMC No. 3740)

Centre Points

Approx stitching time: 15 minutes

{HEART}
29mm (1⅛in) button

9 x 7 stitches

Total stitches: 37

Size on 32-count fabric:
1.4 x 1.1cm (½ x ⅜in)

Allow 1m/39in stranded
cotton @ 2 strands

Colour in photo:
Mocha (Anchor No. 393/
DMC No. 3790)

Centre Points

Approx stitching time: 45 minutes

{BIRD}
38mm (1½in) button

21 x 14 stitches

Total stitches: 113

Size on 32-count fabric:
3.3 x 2.2cm (1¼ x ¾in)

Allow 1.5m/59in stranded
cotton @ 2 strands

Colour in photo:
Shadow (Anchor No. 232/
DMC No. 452)

Miniature Motifs: Embroidered Buttons

55

{practice makes perfect}

The Stag King

JUST LIKE EVERY FAIRY-TALE PLACE that we have ever heard about, over half of Storyland is covered in forest. Naturally, therefore, it is teeming with deer. However, despite their great numbers, these beautiful beasts are rather difficult to spot because they are shy and skittish and incredibly fast. I suppose I would be too if people wanted to hang my head on their wall.

Consequently, it is considered a great achievement to be able to catch a deer. Partly because they are so good at running away, and partly because the majority of Storyland's hunters are galumphing great oafs who do not know the meaning of stealth.

Any deer will do, but the highest prize of all is the Stag King. Between you and me, I'm not entirely convinced he even exists, but the forest folk are adamant. Twice the size of a normal stag and with magnificent oak-like antlers crowning his head, legend says he has walked the forest for centuries and evaded capture by even the most intrepid hunter. Allegedly.

Either way, I rather like the thought of a gigantic, ancient stag roaming the land, in much the same way as I could happily spend days staring into the depths of Loch Ness in the hope of spying its famous monster. So, I would be much obliged if the hunters could kindly clear off and leave the legends be. Thanks ever so.

Stag King Pinboard Hoop

{SUPPLIES}

40.5cm (16in) wooden quilting hoop

Thick, natural cotton fabric (for example heavy calico or raw denim), 50 x 50cm (20 x 20in)

Black tapestry wool, 5m (16½ft)

Large, sharp embroidery needle, size 16 or 18

Fabric scissors or pinking shears

Small, sharp scissors

Clear sticky tape

Black cotton fabric for hoop backing, 50 x 50cm (20 x 20in)

Strong craft glue

Strong dressmaking pins for displaying things on your finished hoop

Pencil

I.
Cut the piece of heavy calico or raw denim fabric a little larger than the diameter of your quilting hoop; approximately 50 x 50cm (20 x 20in).

2.
Iron the fabric carefully to remove any creases, using steam and/or water spray if necessary.

3.
Separate the inner and outer rings of the quilting hoop, place the ironed fabric in between the two rings, push the rings back together and tighten the screw. Pull the fabric taut in the hoop to give a smooth, flat surface by pulling on the edges all around the hoop (see page 14 for more information on using a hoop).

4.
Photocopy the stag chart on page 63 at 200 per cent – you will need to use an A3 photocopier for this. Using a large, sharp embroidery needle, carefully make holes in the four corners of each stitch on the chart.

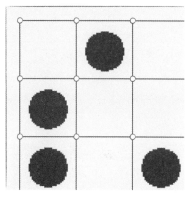

STEP 4

5.

Stick your paper chart in place in the centre of the quilting hoop with sticky tape and, using a sharp pencil, mark dots on the fabric through the holes in the corners of each stitch. You may find it easiest to work through them in rows to ensure you do not miss any.

6.

When you have covered all of the holes, remove the paper chart from the fabric and you will be left with a grid of dots to stitch over.

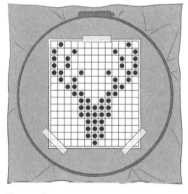

STEP 6

7.

Cut a length of tapestry wool about as long as your arm span and tie a knot in one end. Thread the other end through the eye of your needle.

8.

Using the paper chart as a guide, start stitching your crosses over the grid of dots – the stitching technique is the same as that shown on page 16, just on a much larger scale and using the dots as your grid instead of the holes in the fabric. When you come to the end of a thread, tie another knot on the back of the fabric, pulling it close to the fabric to ensure the final stitch remains tight on the front.

{THIS PROJECT CALLS FOR TAPESTRY WOOL BECAUSE IT IS SO LARGE THAT IT NEEDS SOMETHING THICK AND BULKY TO REALLY PACK A PUNCH AND STAND OUT. STRANDED COTTON HAS A TENDENCY TO UNRAVEL A BIT WHEN IT IS USED FOR SUCH LARGE STITCHES AND REGULAR WOOL IS GENERALLY NOT STRONG ENOUGH TO WITHSTAND BEING DRAGGED THROUGH SMALL HOLES MULTIPLE TIMES WITHOUT FRAYING, SO IT REALLY IS WORTH SEEKING OUT PROPER TAPESTRY WOOL. IT IS SOLD IN SMALL SKEINS (AND IN MANY COLOURS) LIKE EMBROIDERY THREAD SO YOU NEEDN'T BUY AN ENTIRE BALL – MOST PLACES THAT SELL COTTON EMBROIDERY THREAD WILL ALSO STOCK TAPESTRY WOOL.}

9.

Once you have finished stitching, and if you've not already done so, cut a 50 x 50cm (20 x 20in) piece of black cotton fabric for the hoop backing. This will ensure that the backs of your stitches cannot be seen through the light fabric at the front.

10.

Run a line of glue around the outside of the inner hoop ring, stretch the backing fabric over it, tighten the outer ring over the top and pull the fabric taut. Allow the glue to dry.

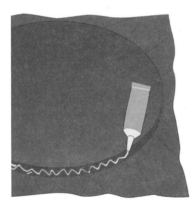

STEP 11

11.

Separate the hoop rings and run another line of glue around the outside of the inner ring, on top of the black fabric.

12.

Stretch the embroidered fabric over the glued black fabric-covered ring so that the back of your embroidery is hidden, then replace and tighten the outer ring again before pulling the excess fabric taut.

13.

When the glue has dried on this second layer, use a pair of small sharp scissors to trim the excess fabric from the back of the hoop.

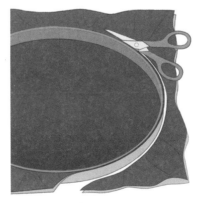

STEP 13

14.

Now your hoop is ready to hang (a nail in the wall will do the trick) and you can use dressmaking pins to attach things to it and/or tuck things into the gigantic cross stitches.

{THERE IS A LOT OF FABRIC INVOLVED IN THIS PROJECT SO WHEN YOU COME TO MOUNT IT IN ITS HOOP IT IS REALLY IMPORTANT TO GIVE THE GLUE PLENTY OF TIME TO DRY BEFORE YOU ADD THE NEXT LAYER OR TRIM THE EXCESS FABRIC – OBVIOUSLY THIS DEPENDS TO A GREAT EXTENT ON THE GLUE YOU ARE USING, BUT IF IN DOUBT IT MAY BE BEST TO LEAVE THE FIRST LAYER TO DRY OVERNIGHT BEFORE MOVING ON TO THE NEXT STEP. IT IS ALSO BEST NOT TO HANG ANYTHING TOO HEAVY FROM YOUR FINISHED PINBOARD HOOP TO KEEP IT LOOKING ITS BEST – IT IS IDEAL FOR DISPLAYING THINGS LIKE CARDS, INVITATIONS AND RIBBONS.}

{STAG KING PATTERN}

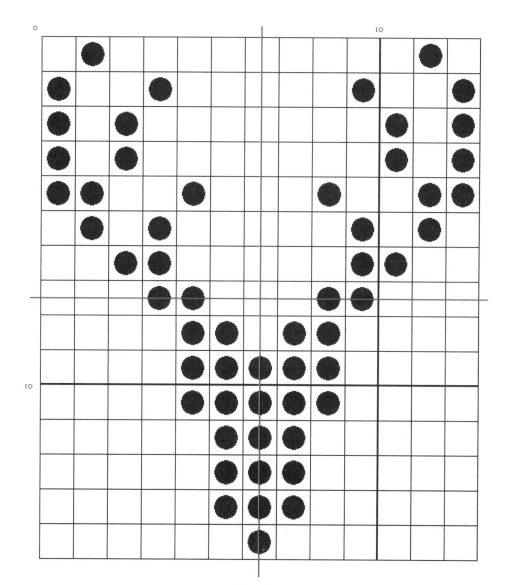

Centre Points

13 x 15 stitches

Total stitches: 56

50% chart size = 12cm wide x 13.84cm high (4³⁄₄in wide x 5½in high)

Photocopy @ 200% to get final chart size of 24cm (9½in) wide x 27.68cm (11in) high (to fit a 40cm/16in hoop)

Thread: Anchor Tapestry Wool (Shade 9800), 1 strand = 5m/16½ft (½ skein)

Approx stitching time: 40 minutes

The Black Cat

IN MY EXPERIENCE people tend to fall into one of two camps: cat people and dog people. I may be betraying my sympathies here, but I have never fully understood why anybody would choose to camp in a place where they end up perpetually covered in dog hair and slobber. However, for some bizarre reason, my friends all seem to disagree. I am convinced this is only because they have never met Amber.

A small black cat who lives with the haggard old witch at the edge of the forest, Amber is almost too clever to be allowed. She can open doors and light fires and run errands: a regular little house elf. Plus, she makes a better guard dog than any canine that I have ever encountered.

You would think that after all this she would be too tired for anything but sleep, and yet, every night when the witch blows out her candle Amber sneaks out of the window, prowls into the forest and is not seen again until dawn.

A few people have commented that Amber has remarkably similar eyes to the witch's daughter – who disappeared a number of years ago following a particularly virulent bout of misbehaviour –
I will leave you to draw your own conclusions.

Black Cat Mask

{SUPPLIES}

Two pieces of thick (1mm+/¹⁄₁₆ in+) black wool felt, 25 x 20cm (10 x 8in) each

14-count waste canvas, 25 x 20cm (10 x 8in)

Stranded cotton embroidery thread in Cream (Anchor No. 926/DMC No. 712) and Pale Peach (Anchor No. 366/ DMC No. 951)

Black sewing thread

Sharp embroidery needle

Small, sharp scissors

Small pair of pliers (optional)

Cream ribbon, 1.2m (48in)

Pins

1.

Cut a piece of felt and a piece of waste canvas to 25 x 20cm (10 x 8in), and then tack them together with a loose running stitch all around the edge.

2.

Follow the instructions on pages 14–15 to find the centre of the fabric and prepare a length of thread – you will need to stitch the design using two strands. You can use a hoop to hold the fabric while you stitch if you find it helpful, but this is not essential.

{WASTE CANVAS IS A TYPE OF EVENWEAVE FABRIC THAT YOU CAN USE TO CROSS STITCH ONTO FABRICS THAT ARE NOT SPECIFICALLY MADE FOR COUNTED EMBROIDERY. IT IS LAYERED ON TOP OF NON-EVENWEAVE FABRICS TO PROVIDE A GUIDE FOR COUNTING AND CAN THEN BE REMOVED FROM UNDERNEATH THE STITCHES WHEN YOU HAVE FINISHED THE DESIGN (SEE STEP 4). WASTE CANVAS CAN BE SUBSTITUTED FOR SOLUBLE CANVAS IF YOU PREFER – SEE PAGE 82 FOR INFORMATION ON SOLUBLE CANVAS.}

3.

Working from the centre point outwards, follow the pattern on pages 70–71 to stitch the mask.

4.

When you have finished stitching, you will need to remove the waste canvas. First remove the tacking stitches from around the edge, and then spray with water before removing each thread from the waste canvas, one at a time. The easiest way to do this is to use a small pair of pliers to grip the threads, but you can also do it by hand. When you have removed all the threads, lay the felt flat on a towel to dry naturally.

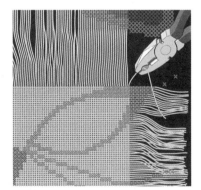

STEP 4

5.

Photocopy and cut out the template opposite. Pin the template over your embroidered felt, aligning the eyes to ensure everything is in the right place underneath. Then, using a pair of small, sharp scissors, carefully cut the felt to the shape of the template.

6.

To cut out the eyes, fold the mask and make a cut in the middle of the first eye – you can then insert your scissors through the hole and follow the line of the embroidery, cutting a few millimetres (sixteenths of an inch) inside the stitches to shape the eye. Repeat with the other eye.

STEP 6

7.

Pin the mask onto a second piece of black felt and use it as a template to carefully cut a duplicate shape out of the felt for the mask backing.

8.

Cut two lengths of ribbon to 60cm (23¾in) each. Place the plain felt shape behind the embroidered one and then insert the end of one of the ribbons between the two pieces of felt at the widest part of the cheek. Place a pin through both layers of felt with the ribbon in the middle to hold it in place.

9.

Repeat the process in step 8 to insert the other ribbon into the opposite side of the mask.

10.

Pin around the rest of the mask edges to join the two pieces of felt, then, using a sharp needle (your embroidery needle will do) with some black sewing thread, sew a small, neat running stitch all around the edge of the mask, and around the insides of the eyes. Sew a couple of extra rows of stitches over the ribbons to ensure they are attached securely to the mask.

11.

All that remains is to tidy up the ends of the ribbons so that they don't fray. Fold each ribbon in half lengthwise about 2.5cm (1in) from the end, and use a pair of small, sharp scissors to cut through the folded ribbon at an angle – cut upwards from the edges of the ribbon to the highest point on the fold. Now your mask is ready to wear!

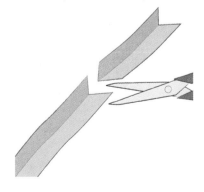

STEP 11

Centre Points

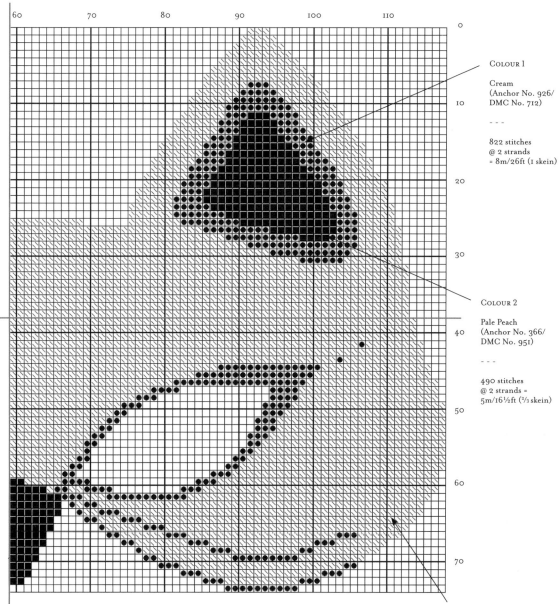

60   70   80   90   100   110   0

COLOUR 1

Cream
(Anchor No. 926/
DMC No. 712)

10

- - -

822 stitches
@ 2 strands
= 8m/26ft (1 skein)

20

30

COLOUR 2

Pale Peach
(Anchor No. 366/
DMC No. 951)

40

- - -

490 stitches
@ 2 strands =
5m/16½ft (²⁄₃ skein)

50

60

70

SECTION 3

{YOU MAY FIND IT EASIER TO PHOTOCOPY THIS CHART,

STICK THE SEPARATE SECTIONS TOGETHER AND THEN MARK

OFF EACH SECTION AS YOU STITCH. COPY AT AN INCREASED

SIZE IF YOU PREFER TO WORK FROM A LARGER PATTERN.}

These symbols need not
be stitched – they simply
show the outline shape
of the mask (which you
can cut to size using the
template when you have
finished stitching).

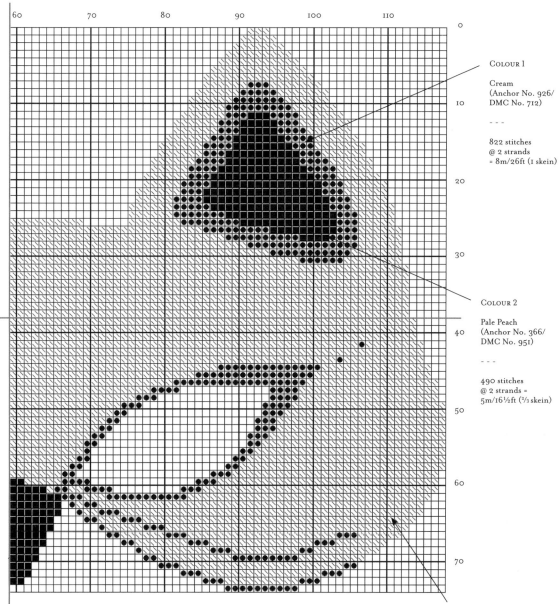

Black Cat Mask

The Princess & the Knight

NO ANCIENT LAND worth its salt is complete without a princess, and Storyland is lucky enough to boast an especially formidable one. In the absence of a male heir, she took it upon herself to become as bold and brave as the best of men. However, admirable as this was, it meant that when it came to finding a husband, things were not quite as straightforward as they might otherwise have been.

For years she scorned the painted peacocks who paraded through the court, each as weak and spineless as the one before, perpetually impressed with their own self-importance. She had her eye on someone else. A delicious, rugged, axe-wielding, woodcutter who lived in the woods outside the castle walls. He was entirely unsuitable, of course: brash and poor and unrefined. But that just made the princess more determined to get her own way. Tantrums and protests ensued, but the king still refused to accept the union. Then fate intervened and the woodcutter was given a chance to prove his worth when a dragon took it upon himself to steal the princess away.

I am inclined to believe that the princess may have had a hand in this 'fateful' occurrence, since I am sure she could have given the dragon a run for his money herself, but to this day she denies any involvement. Anyway, the woodcutter succeeded in 'rescuing' the princess when all others failed and the king had no choice but to knight the woodcutter for his skill and daring, and allow him to marry his daughter. Finally, the princess had found a man as courageous and brave as she was.

Lord help anyone who gets in their way.

Cameo Frames: the Princess & the Knight

{SUPPLIES}

2 pieces of 28-count cream linen, 35 x 45cm (13¾ x 17¾in) each

Stranded cotton embroidery thread in black, 67m (220ft)

Tapestry needle, size 24 or 26

Small, sharp scissors

2 picture frames with 20 x 25.5cm (8 x 10in) apertures; glass is optional

A3 sheet of cream mount board

Pencil

Craft knife and cutting mat

Sewing thread for framing

1.
Following the instructions on pages 14–15, prepare one of the pieces of linen and a length of thread for the first cameo – you will need a thread thickness of three strands to stitch each pattern if you are using stranded cotton thread. You can use a frame to hold the fabric while you stitch if you find it helpful, but this is not essential.

2.
Follow the pattern on page 78 to stitch the first design. When this is finished, repeat the process with the pattern on page 79, stitching the second pattern onto the remaining piece of linen.

3.
When you have finished stitching both cameos, carefully handwash the fabric, if necessary, and then iron it face down over a towel to protect the stitches, so that the cameos are ready for framing.

4.
Remove the back of the first picture frame, and make sure that the frame is clean (and the glass, too, if you are keeping it in). These frames were a very gaudy gold to start with so they have been painted black – you can customise yours in whatever way you wish. Once you have cleaned/painted the frames, you can set them to one side for the time being.

5.

You will need to stretch your embroidery over a piece of mount board to keep it in place and flat in the frame. The mount board needs to be the same size and shape as the slot behind the opening in the frame. Usually, picture frames come with a piece of paper inside that has been placed into the frame for display in the shop. You can use this as a template to cut your piece of mount board to size. Use the template to mark the shape on your sheet of mount board with a pencil (making sure you leave enough space to cut the board for the second frame too).

6.

Carefully cut out the shape on the mount board with a craft knife, running a couple of millimetres inside the line to allow for the extra bulk of fabric that will be folded around the board. Mount board is very thick and you will need to press quite hard with the knife, so a cutting mat is essential.

7.

Place the shaped mount board over the top of your stitched linen and use a pencil to mark a cutting line approximately 5cm (2in) larger than the mount board all the way around the fabric (see below).

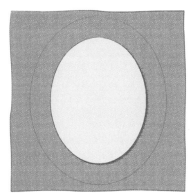

STEP 7

8.

Cut the fabric around the line you have just made and then place it face down on a flat surface with the mount board on top. The cream side of the mount board should be face down, the same way as the fabric, so that it fills any gaps in the linen with matching colour.

9.

With a double thickness of sewing thread, make a knot in the middle of one edge of the linen and then lace the two edges from side to side over the mount board like a corset, pulling the thread tight so that it stretches the stitched design on the front of the board.

10.

Lace all the way along the length of the mount board, working from the middle outwards and changing the thread as needed (see below).

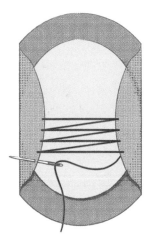

STEP 10

11.

Repeat the process to lace the top and bottom edges of linen together.

12.

Place your mounted embroidery in the frame and seal the back. Repeat steps 4 to 12 to frame the second cross-stitched cameo.

{I GENERALLY PREFER TO FRAME MY EMBROIDERY WITHOUT GLASS BECAUSE OVER A PERIOD OF TIME IT HAS A TENDENCY TO CRUSH THE STITCHES. IF YOU BUY FROM A SPECIALIST FRAME SHOP THE GLASS IS GENERALLY SOLD SEPARATELY ANYWAY, SO YOU HAVE A LOT MORE CHOICE. IF YOU PREFER TO USE GLASS, IT IS BEST TO CHOOSE A BOX-STYLE FRAME WHERE THE FABRIC IS SET BACK FROM THE GLASS AND DOES NOT TOUCH IT.}

{THE KNIGHT PATTERN}

Centre Points

65 x 94 stitches

Total stitches: 3,653

Design size on 28-count linen:
11.8 x 17.1cm (4½ x 6½in)

Allow 37m/122ft thread
(using 3 strands)

{THE PRINCESS PATTERN}

Centre Points

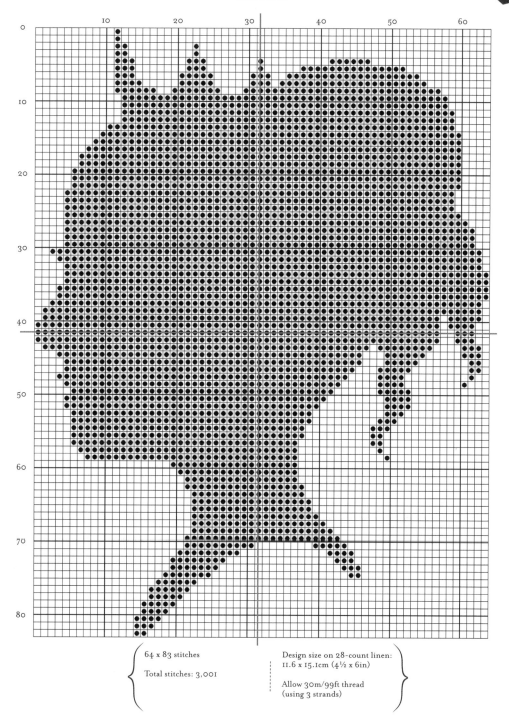

64 x 83 stitches

Total stitches: 3,001

Design size on 28-count linen:
11.6 x 15.1cm (4½ x 6in)

Allow 30m/99ft thread
(using 3 strands)

Coat of Arms

HE KING MAY HAVE eventually allowed his daughter to marry a humble woodcutter-turned-knight, but he was not about to let his royal coat of arms be besmirched by an alliance with common blood.

Therefore, under the guise of generosity, as part of their marriage settlement the princess and the knight were granted their very own coat of arms by the king.

Heraldry relies upon the use of symbols to express a noble family's history and heritage, and, as such, this new coat of arms would tell the story of the couple's union.

The crown to signify the princess' royal blood; the axe and the arrow, the couple's weapons of choice; the tree, a symbol of the forest in which they met; the lightning, the princess' temper and spirit; the star representing the alignment of the fates that brought the pair together; and above all lays the heart, for true love.

It shall be the foundation of a new dynasty.

Coat of Arms Book Cover

{SUPPLIES}

Two pieces of thick (1mm+/¹⁄₁₆ in+) wool felt in charcoal, 50 x 21cm (20 x 8¼in), and in burgundy 13 x 18cm (5¼ x 7in)

14-count soluble canvas, 12 x 16cm (4¾ x 6¼in)

Stranded cotton embroidery threads in Cream (Anchor No. 926/DMC No. 712) and Metallic Gold (Kreinik Fine Braid #8)

Grey and burgundy sewing threads

Sharp embroidery needle

Small, sharp scissors

Pins

1.
Cut a 13 x 18cm (5¼ x 7in) piece of burgundy felt and a slightly smaller 12 x 16cm (4¾ x 6¼in) piece of soluble canvas.

2.
Follow the instructions on page 15 to find the centre of the soluble canvas and mark it with a pin or needle. Place the soluble canvas on top of the felt and tack the two pieces of fabric together with a loose running stitch around the edge.

3.
Prepare a length of thread (see page 15). This design uses two types of thread: Stranded Cotton is stitched using two strands; if you are using Kreinik Fine Braid #8 for the metallic gold you will need to stitch these sections with a single strand. You can use a hoop to hold the fabric while you stitch if you find it helpful, but this is not essential.

4.
Working from the centre point outwards, follow the pattern on page 85 to stitch the coat of arms.

5.
When you have finished stitching, remove the tacking stitches joining the two fabrics together and place the felt upside down in a bowl of lukewarm water for 10 minutes to dissolve the soluble canvas. Allow the felt to dry naturally (be careful where you put it as a little dye may come out of the felt).

6.
When the felt is dry, cut around your embroidery a few millimetres from the outer stitches.

{SOLUBLE CANVAS IS A TYPE OF EVENWEAVE FABRIC THAT YOU CAN USE TO CROSS STITCH ONTO FABRICS THAT ARE NOT SPECIFICALLY MADE FOR COUNTED EMBROIDERY. IT IS LAYERED ON TOP OF NON-EVENWEAVE FABRICS TO PROVIDE A GUIDE FOR COUNTING AND CAN THEN BE DISSOLVED FROM UNDERNEATH THE STITCHES WHEN YOU HAVE FINISHED THE DESIGN (SEE STEP 5). SOLUBLE CANVAS CAN BE SUBSTITUTED FOR WASTE CANVAS IF YOU PREFER – SEE PAGE 66 FOR INFORMATION ON WASTE CANVAS.}

Big Bad Wolf Pencil Case

{SUPPLIES}

**2 pieces of 32-count natural/
raw linen, 30 x 22cm
(12 x 8¾in) each**

**Cotton/calico lining fabric,
30 x 60cm (12 x 24in)**

**Stranded cotton embroidery
threads in Blue/Grey (Anchor
No. 401/DMC No. 413),
Cream (Anchor No. 926/
DMC No. 712) and Gold
(Kreinik Fine Braid #8)**

Tapestry needle, size 26 or 28

Small, sharp scissors

20cm (8in) trouser zip

**Sewing machine or needle with
cream and taupe sewing threads**

Pins

I.
Cut two pieces of linen to 30 x 22cm
(12 x 8¾in).

2.
Follow the instructions on pages 14–15
to prepare one of the pieces of fabric,
find its centre point and prepare a
length of thread. The design uses
two types of thread: Stranded Cotton
is stitched using two strands; if you are
using Kreinik Fine Braid #8 for the
metallic gold, you will need to stitch
these sections with a single strand. You
can use a hoop to hold the fabric while
you stitch if you find it helpful, but
this is not essential.

3.
Working from the centre point
outwards, follow the pattern on pages
94–95 to stitch the wolf and border.

4.
When you have finished stitching,
carefully handwash the fabric, if
necessary, and iron it face down over
a towel; this will act as a cushion to
protect your stitches. If you wish, you
could stitch some initials onto the
second piece of linen to personalise
the design (you could use letters from
the sampler pattern on pages 136–137
for this). Alternatively, leave the
second piece of linen blank and iron.

5.
If you want to make your pencil case
more rigid, at this point you need to
fix some iron-on backing fabric to
the two pieces of linen. All fabrics
are slightly different, so you will
need to follow the manufacturer's
instructions for your specific one.
Cut the backing fabric slightly smaller
than the pieces of linen and bond it
to the back of the linen with an iron.
If you want your case to be more
flexible, then skip this step.

6.

Place the two pieces of linen together, right sides in. On the top edge of your linen, centre the zip and mark with a pencil the two points where the zip's teeth end.

STEP 6

7.

With a 1cm (⅜in) seam allowance, sew along the top edge from one corner to the first point you marked, securing the loose thread with a couple of backstitches. Repeat for the opposite side. Press the seams open all along the top edge.

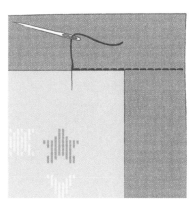

STEP 7

8.

Pin the zip (face down) between the two edges you have just sewn together at the ends – the two sides of the zip should be attached to separate pieces of fabric either side of the gap in the middle.

9.

Sew all the way around the edge of the zip with taupe-coloured thread, as shown below (you will be able to see it on the front of the case, so keep it neat!). If you are using a sewing machine with a regular foot attachment, you will need to push it right up against the zip and move the zip-pull back and forth to make space for the foot either side of it. Secure the loose thread end with a couple of backstitches. You should be left with a covered zip when you turn the fabric the right way out.

STEP 9

10.

Cut two pieces of cotton/calico lining fabric to 30 x 22cm (12 x 8¾in) each. For each piece of fabric, make a 1cm (⅜in) fold along one of the 30cm (12in) edges and press into place.

11.

Now cut two 5 x 5cm (2 x 2in) pieces of lining fabric and again fold and press one of the edges to give each piece of fabric a 1cm (⅜in) flap along one side.

12.

Place the zipped fabric pieces face down and line up the four pieces of cotton/calico on top.

13.

Place the two smallest pieces of fabric at either end of the zip to cover the open ends, then put the two larger pieces along the length of the zip on either side, aligning them with the embroidered layers below. The folded edges should all be touching the zip with their flaps facing down (see below).

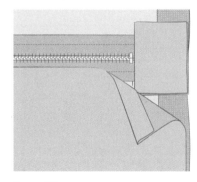

STEP 13

14.

Using cream sewing thread and a neat running stitch, hand sew the four pieces of lining to the very edge of the zip – this part is a little fiddly but the lining is essential to hide any raw edges and make sure your case is strong enough to withstand frequent use (see below).

STEP 14

15.

When attaching the larger pieces, lift them up so that you can see the 1cm (³⁄₈in) flap and sew right along the fold you made earlier; to attach the small end pieces you will need to sew a neat line over the top (see below). You can secure the loose thread with a couple of backstitches or a knot between the linen and the lining.

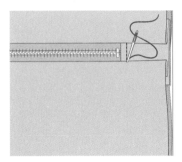

16.

It is very important that you open the zip before this next step! If you leave the zip closed, you will not be able to turn your case the right way out. Now arrange the four pieces of fabric so that the two pieces of lining are facing each other and the two pieces of linen are facing each other (see right). At this point you should not be able to see the zip at all. Pin the three open edges of the linen together, and use taupe thread to sew a 1cm (³⁄₈in) seam around them. Secure the loose threads at each end with a couple of backstitches.

Step 16

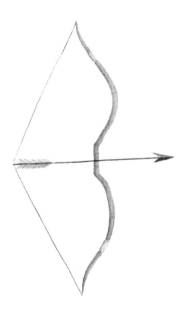

17.

Snip the four corners of the lining, taking care not to cut into the seams. As you did with the linen, align the two pieces of cotton/calico lining and pin them together along the two sides, but this time leave the bottom edge open. When pinning the top of the lining nearest to the zip, fold the small pieces of fabric (that were used to cover the ends of the zip) flat in half around the top of the main lining (see below).

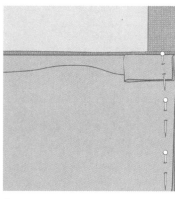

STEP 17

18.

Use cream thread to sew the lining together with a 1cm (⅜in) seam along each pinned side. Leave the bottom of the lining completely open.

19.

Snip the four corners of the linen, taking care not to cut into the seams. Put your hands through the open bottom edge and then through the open zip to turn the linen right side out and poke out the corners. Leave the lining hanging out of the open zip.

STEP 19

20.

Fold and press the raw edges of the open side of the lining inwards, then pin them together. Sew together with a neat topstitch using cream thread. The closer you can make the topstitch to the edge of the fabric, the neater it will look.

21.

Secure the loose threads with a couple of backstitches before weaving the ends between the outer fabric and the lining. Push the lining inside the zip and fill your case with lovely things.

{IF ADDING A LINING SEEMS TOO COMPLICATED, YOU COULD INSTEAD MAKE A MUCH SIMPLER VERSION OF THIS ZIPPED CASE USING FELT IN PLACE OF THE LINEN BECAUSE IT DOES NOT FRAY. THE INSTRUCTIONS ON PAGES 66 AND 82 WILL SHOW YOU HOW TO STITCH ONTO THE FELT USING 14-COUNT WASTE CANVAS OR SOLUBLE CANVAS (THIS WILL MAKE THE CASE A LITTLE LARGER). WHEN YOU HAVE FINISHED STITCHING THE FELT, TO MAKE IT INTO A CASE FOLLOW STEPS 6–9 IN THIS PROJECT, THEN SKIP TO STEPS 16 AND 17, IGNORING ANY MENTION OF THE LINING FABRIC. TURN THE CASE OUT THE RIGHT WAY AND YOU'RE DONE – EASY AS PIE!}

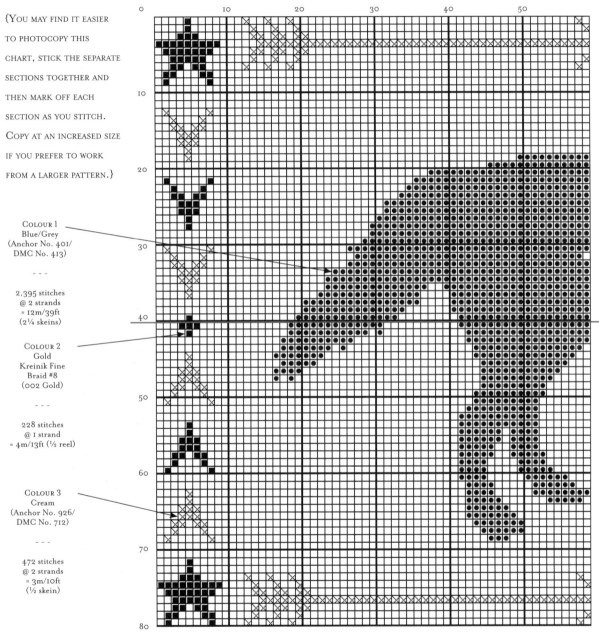

{THE BIG BAD WOLF PATTERN – PART I}

{YOU MAY FIND IT EASIER
TO PHOTOCOPY THIS
CHART, STICK THE SEPARATE
SECTIONS TOGETHER AND
THEN MARK OFF EACH
SECTION AS YOU STITCH.
COPY AT AN INCREASED SIZE
IF YOU PREFER TO WORK
FROM A LARGER PATTERN.}

COLOUR 1
Blue/Grey
(Anchor No. 401/
DMC No. 413)

- - -

2,395 stitches
@ 2 strands
= 12m/39ft
(2¼ skeins)

COLOUR 2
Gold
Kreinik Fine
Braid #8
(002 Gold)

- - -

228 stitches
@ 1 strand
= 4m/13ft (½ reel)

COLOUR 3
Cream
(Anchor No. 926/
DMC No. 712)

- - -

472 stitches
@ 2 strands
= 3m/10ft
(½ skein)

{THE BIG BAD WOLF PATTERN - PART 2}

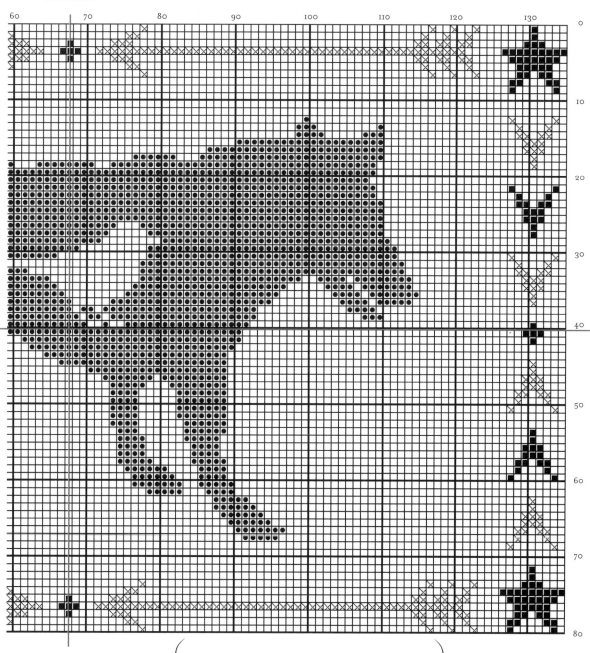

Centre Points

135 x 80 stitches

Total stitches: 3,095

Design size on 32-count linen:
21.4 x 12.7cm (8½ x 5in)

{ projects for the brave } & determined

The Wise Owl

I WAS BORN OLD, and, despite my best efforts, I have never been very good at acting my age. I think this is one of the reasons why I have such an affinity with this wise old bird.

When I was a child and we had a house full of people, I rarely played with the other children for long. Instead, I used to sit so silent and still in the corner of a room full of grown-ups that they would forget that I was there. Consequently, they would talk about all sorts of things that I probably shouldn't have been listening to, and I would hear everything. Most excellent.

People often overlook small ears but they understand considerably more than you would think, which is exactly how our owl came to be so wise. For years he has perched in the top of the tallest tree, silently taking in everything that goes on below. He doesn't gossip, he doesn't interfere; he just watches and listens and remembers everything.

And I mean everything.

If you are looking for counsel you will find nobody better.

Twit twoo.

Wise Owl Pillow

{SUPPLIES}

**28-count cream linen,
30 x 40cm (12 x 16in)**

**Stranded cotton embroidery
thread in Chocolate (Anchor
No. 360/DMC No. 898),
Cumin (Anchor No. 365/
DMC No. 435) and Cinnamon
(Anchor No. 370/DMC No. 434)**

Tapestry needle, size 24 or 26

Small, sharp scissors

**2 pieces of natural calico or
similar cotton backing fabric,
30 x 40cm (12 x 16in)**

Pencil

**Sewing machine or needle
and cream sewing thread**

Cushion stuffing

I.

Cut a piece of linen to 30 x 40cm
(12 x 16in).

2.

Follow the instructions on pages 14–15
to prepare your evenweave fabric, find
its centre point and prepare a length
of thread – you will need to stitch the
design using three strands. You can
use a hoop or roller frame to hold the
fabric while you stitch if you find it
helpful, but this is not essential.

3.

Working from the centre point
outwards, follow the pattern on
pages 102–103 to stitch the owl.

4.

When you have finished stitching,
carefully handwash the fabric, if
necessary, and iron it face down over
a towel; this will act as a cushion
to protect your stitches.

5.

On the back of your linen fabric
mark a line around the stitched
design, adding approximately 8cm
(3$\frac{1}{8}$in) around all the edges of your
embroidery and leaving the bottom
edge flat but with rounded corners.

Step 5

6.

Cut around the marked line and use it as a template to mark two more identical shapes onto the calico fabric. Cut the two calico shapes out too.

7.

Position one of the calico shapes on a table, place your embroidered linen on top of it (face up) and layer the second calico shape on the top so that your embroidery is sandwiched in the middle. Pin the three layers together.

STEP 7

8.

Using a sewing machine or needle and thread, sew the three layers together, approximately 1cm (⅜in) from the edge, leaving an 8–10cm (3⅛–4in) section in the middle of the flat bottom edge open so that you can turn the shape the right way out. Secure the loose ends with a couple of backstitches.

9.

Cut notches around the curves in the edge, taking care not to cut into the seams. Then press the seams open with an iron.

STEP 9

10.

Turn the shape out the right way so that the embroidery is facing out and the two pieces of calico are together. Fill the hollow between the two pieces of calico with stuffing. Stuff as much as you can into the hole, pushing it right to the edges to make sure your pillow is nice and plump.

11.

Neatly sew the open seam closed by hand, secure the thread with a couple of backstitches and weave the loose end between the layers of fabric.

(AS AN ALTERNATIVE TO THIS SHAPED PILLOW, YOU COULD EASILY TURN THIS DESIGN INTO A REGULAR SQUARE OR RECTANGULAR CUSHION. MAKING UP INSTRUCTIONS FOR AN ENVELOPE-BACK CUSHION CAN BE FOUND ON PAGES 120–121 – YOU WILL JUST NEED TO ADJUST THE MEASUREMENTS TO FIT YOUR CHOSEN CUSHION PAD. MAKE SURE YOU LEAVE PLENTY OF ROOM AROUND THE EDGE OF THE PATTERN FOR MAKING UP THE CUSHION. THE MEASUREMENTS OF THE FINISHED STITCHING CAN BE FOUND ON THE PATTERN ON PAGE 102.)

{WISE OWL PATTERN}

Approx
stitching
time:
22½
hours

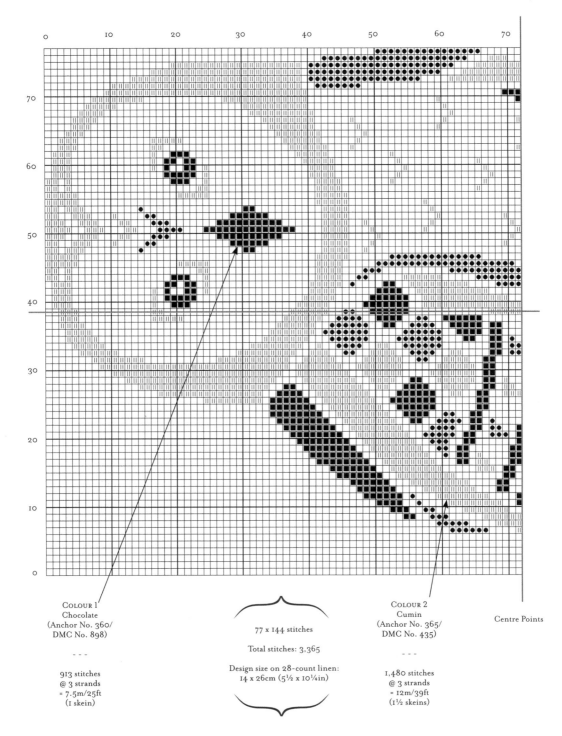

COLOUR 1
Chocolate
(Anchor No. 360/
DMC No. 898)

- - -

913 stitches
@ 3 strands
= 7.5m/25ft
(1 skein)

77 x 144 stitches

Total stitches: 3,365

Design size on 28-count linen:
14 x 26cm (5½ x 10¼in)

COLOUR 2
Cumin
(Anchor No. 365/
DMC No. 435)

- - -

1,480 stitches
@ 3 strands
= 12m/39ft
(1½ skeins)

Centre Points

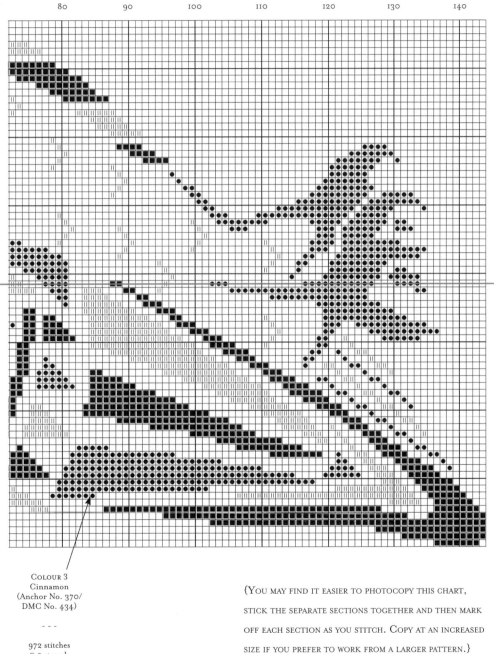

COLOUR 3
Cinnamon
(Anchor No. 370/
DMC No. 434)

- - -

972 stitches
@ 3 strands
= 8m/26ft
(1 skein)

{YOU MAY FIND IT EASIER TO PHOTOCOPY THIS CHART,
STICK THE SEPARATE SECTIONS TOGETHER AND THEN MARK
OFF EACH SECTION AS YOU STITCH. COPY AT AN INCREASED
SIZE IF YOU PREFER TO WORK FROM A LARGER PATTERN.}

The Enchanted Forest

YOU MAY NOT KNOW THIS, but not every forest is enchanted. This is a constant source of irritation to me, because I have always wanted some magical woodland friends to spend my time with, but no matter how many times I visit my local forest, it simply refuses to be anything but normal.

Imagine my excitement, then, when the delightful Mr Fox spirited me away on a magical mystery tour to meet some of his friends in just such a place. According to him, enchanted forests are never easy to get to – apparently it is a basic entry requirement that you must be able to work out the path for yourself. Or else that you at least have the initiative to cheat and get someone else to show you the way...

At first it seems just like any other forest, except for a strange feeling in the air: a sort of tingling that permeates your skin. Then up you look and in the gloaming they stand, at the point where oak meets maple and ivy, under the shade of an enormous gnarled and twisted skeleton of a tree: unicorn and jackalope and frog-prince.

They can all talk, of course, (I would expect nothing less in an enchanted forest), and they really do make rather splendid company. Though I am not convinced that the frog is truly a prince, because when I kissed him nothing happened. Also, I think he may have stolen that crown from the fairies. If I'm honest, however, even as a regular frog he was preferable to some of the men I have kissed, so I think I can live with the disappointment.

C'est la vie.

Enchanted Forest Hoop Cluster

{SUPPLIES}

Wooden embroidery hoops:
2 x 30cm (12in), 2 x 18cm (7in),
2 x 12.5cm (5in), 1 x 10cm (4in)

1 square metre (10 square feet)
of 32-count evenweave fabric,
cream

100m (330ft) of stranded cotton
embroidery thread in black

1 square metre (10 square feet)
of cream backing fabric, such
as calico

Tapestry needle, size 24 or 26

Craft glue

Small, sharp scissors

1.
Begin by cutting seven smaller squares from the evenweave fabric as shown in the diagram opposite.

2.
Follow the instructions on pages 14–15 to prepare the square of evenweave fabric and the length of thread for the first pattern you wish to stitch, fixing the fabric into the hoop size as shown in the diagram opposite.

3.
Follow the patterns on pages 109–113 to stitch each design in its hoop. You will need a thread thickness of three strands to stitch all seven patterns.

4.
When you have finished stitching each design, remove the fabric from its hoop and gently handwash, if necessary. Then iron face down over a towel to protect the stitches, so that it is ready for framing.

5.
To frame each design in its hoop, cut a square of backing fabric to roughly the same size as the piece of stitched evenweave you are working on, ironing it if necessary to remove any bumps or creases. Then separate the two rings of the hoop and run a thin line of glue around the outside of the inner ring.

6.

Stretch the backing fabric over the inner ring, and tighten the outer ring over the top to bond the fabric to the wood, pulling the backing fabric taut to give a smooth, flat surface.

7.

Once the glue is dry enough to hold the backing fabric in place, remove the outer ring and run another thin line of glue around the inner ring, over the top of the backing fabric, in the same way as you did in step 4. If the glue is too thick, it will spread and show on the fabric at the front, so take extra care.

1m (39in)

50 x 50cm (20 x 20in)
To use in 30cm (12in) hoop
for Twig Tree

50 x 50cm (20 x 20in)
To use in 30cm (12in) hoop
for Unicorn

1m (39in)

30 x 30cm (12 x 12in)
To use in 18cm (7in)
hoop for Jackalope

30 x 30cm (12 x 12in)
To use in 18cm (7in)
hoop for Frog Prince

20 x 20cm
(8 x 8in)
To use in
12.5cm (5in)
hoop
for Maple Leaf

20 x 20cm
(8 x 8in)
To use in
12.5cm (5in)
hoop
for Oak Leaf

20 x 20cm
(8 x 8in)
To use in
10cm (4in) hoop
for Ivy Leaf

8.

Align the embroidered evenweave fabric over the top of the backing fabric and inner ring, and stretch it over the edges, again covering with the outer ring to bond the fabrics together. Once you have tightened the outer ring, pull the excess fabric taut to flatten and smooth the fabric visible in the hoop before the glue dries.

9.

Once the glue has dried you can trim the two layers of excess fabric at the back of the hoop with a sharp pair of scissors, cutting as close to the wood as you are able. Et voilà!

10.

The hoop is now ready to hang on a nail or with a couple of blobs of adhesive putty on the back. Repeat the above steps for each hoop and arrange them on your wall.

{UNICORN PATTERN}

Centre Points

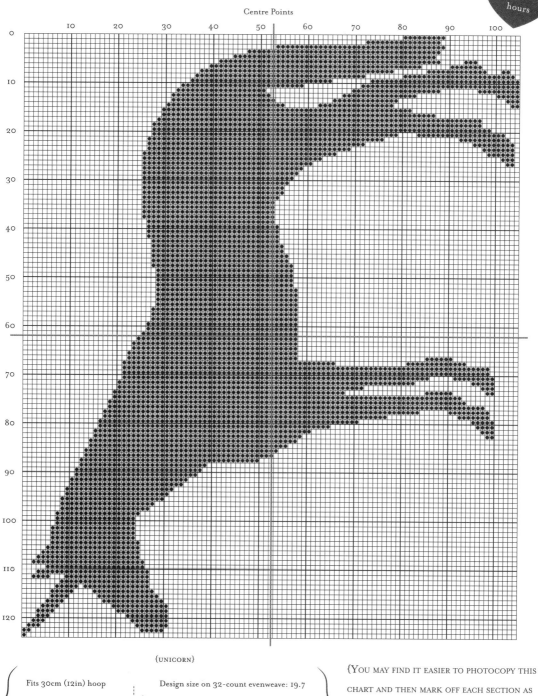

{UNICORN}

Fits 30cm (12in) hoop

124 x 105 stitches

Total stitches: 4,492

Design size on 32-count evenweave: 19.7 x 16.7cm (7¾ x 6½in)

Allow 30m/99ft thread (using 3 strands)

{YOU MAY FIND IT EASIER TO PHOTOCOPY THIS CHART AND THEN MARK OFF EACH SECTION AS YOU STITCH. COPY AT AN INCREASED SIZE IF YOU PREFER TO WORK FROM A LARGER PATTERN.}

{FROG PRINCE PATTERN}

Approx stitching time: 16½ hours

Centre Points

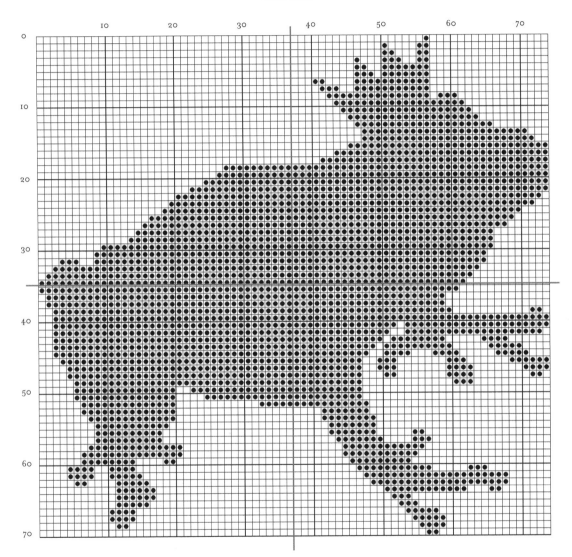

{FROG PRINCE}

Fits 18cm (7in) hoop

74 x 70 stitches

Total stitches: 2,479

Design size on 32-count evenweave: 11.7 x 11.1cm (4½ x 4⅓ in)

Allow 16m/53ft thread (using 3 strands)

{JACKALOPE PATTERN}

Centre Points

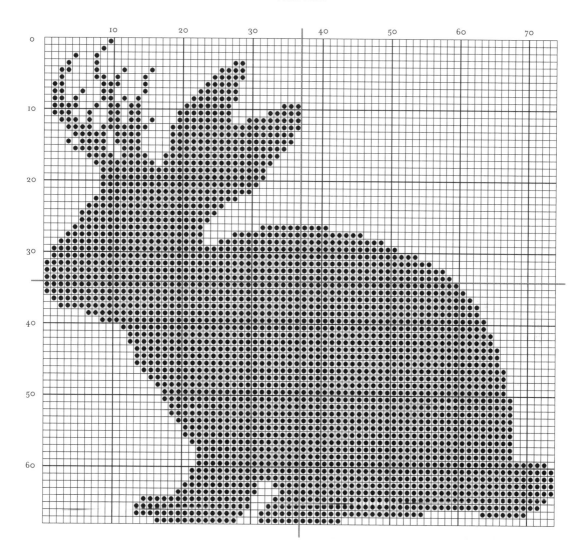

{JACKALOPE}

Fits 18cm (7in) hoop

74 x 68 stitches

Total stitches: 2,610

Design size on 32-count evenweave:
11.7 x 10.8cm (4½ x 4¼in)

Allow 17m/56ft thread
(using 3 strands)

{TWIG TREE PATTERN}

Centre Points

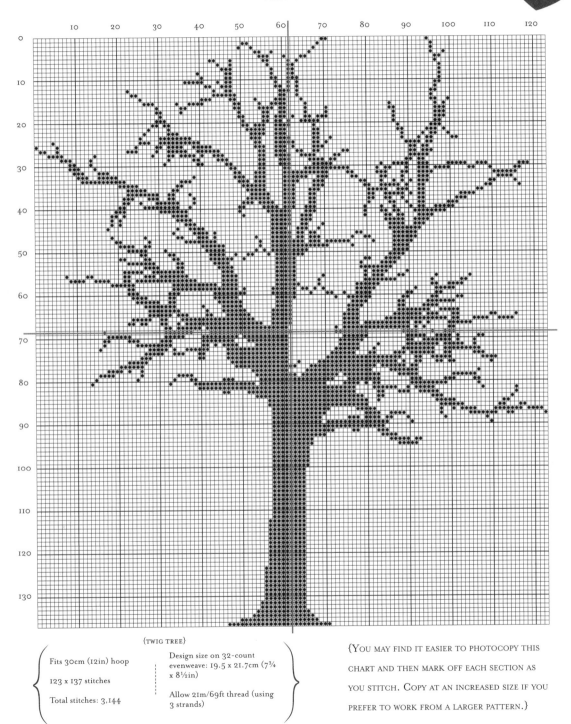

(TWIG TREE)

Fits 30cm (12in) hoop

123 x 137 stitches

Total stitches: 3,144

Design size on 32-count evenweave: 19.5 x 21.7cm (7¾ x 8½in)

Allow 21m/69ft thread (using 3 strands)

{YOU MAY FIND IT EASIER TO PHOTOCOPY THIS CHART AND THEN MARK OFF EACH SECTION AS YOU STITCH. COPY AT AN INCREASED SIZE IF YOU PREFER TO WORK FROM A LARGER PATTERN.}

{3 LEAVES PATTERNS}

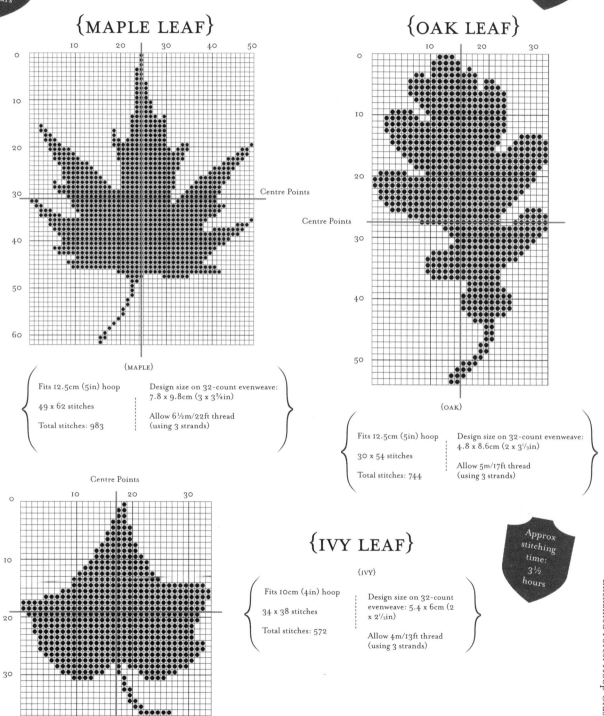

{MAPLE LEAF}

Centre Points

{MAPLE}

Fits 12.5cm (5in) hoop

49 x 62 stitches

Total stitches: 983

Design size on 32-count evenweave: 7.8 x 9.8cm (3 x 3¾in)

Allow 6½m/22ft thread (using 3 strands)

{OAK LEAF}

Centre Points

{OAK}

Fits 12.5cm (5in) hoop

30 x 54 stitches

Total stitches: 744

Design size on 32-count evenweave: 4.8 x 8.6cm (2 x 3⅓in)

Allow 5m/17ft thread (using 3 strands)

Centre Points

Centre Points

{IVY LEAF}

{IVY}

Fits 10cm (4in) hoop

34 x 38 stitches

Total stitches: 572

Design size on 32-count evenweave: 5.4 x 6cm (2 x 2⅓in)

Allow 4m/13ft thread (using 3 strands)

Enchanted Forest Hoop Cluster

Off with their Heads!

BAD THINGS HAVE A WAY of happening to good people. This is unfortunate but true. And so it came to pass that when our jolly but mischievous frog prince played a little prank on the queen, she suffered a severe sense-of-humour bypass.

The unicorn and jackalope leapt in and attempted to salvage the situation, but to no avail: all three found themselves a head shorter.

Nobody knows exactly what happened to leave the queen quite so riled because she has since forbidden any mention of it, but rumours abound that it involved a rather rude sign, some fairy dust, a pair of flowery knickers, a large net and a trumpet…

I shall leave you to draw your own conclusions.

Enchanted Forest Miniatures

{SUPPLIES}

For each head you will need:

At least 20 x 20cm (8 x 8in) of cotton evenweave fabric – either 27- or 28- count, ivory/cream

2 x 8m (26ft) skeins of stranded cotton embroidery thread in black

20 x 20cm (8 x 8in) of cream backing fabric, such as calico

Wooden embroidery hoop, 12.5cm (5in)

Tapestry needle, size 24

Craft glue

Small, sharp scissors

As unfortunate as this series of events may be, it offers me the perfect opportunity to show you how you can adapt my patterns to suit yourself.

For example, the Enchanted Forest Hoop Cluster we have just seen is incredibly lovely, but not everybody has the time or inclination to spend that long stitching a single project. Here I have simply lopped the heads off three of the designs to create much smaller patterns that are simpler and faster to stitch. I have also stitched them onto fabric with a larger weave/lower thread count so that they end up a bit bigger and are nice and easy for beginners.

There is no law that says you should stitch a pattern or project exactly as it is – once you have learned the basics, then feel free to break the rules! You can change colours, stitch onto different fabrics, or mix up sections from different patterns until you have a project that is truly individual.

Each head fits into a 12.5cm (5in) wooden hoop and the instructions at the start of the book will show you how to stitch it. You will need a thread thickness of four strands to stitch all three patterns. You can then follow the steps on pages 106–108 to frame it in its hoop.

Now you just need to decide which one to make!

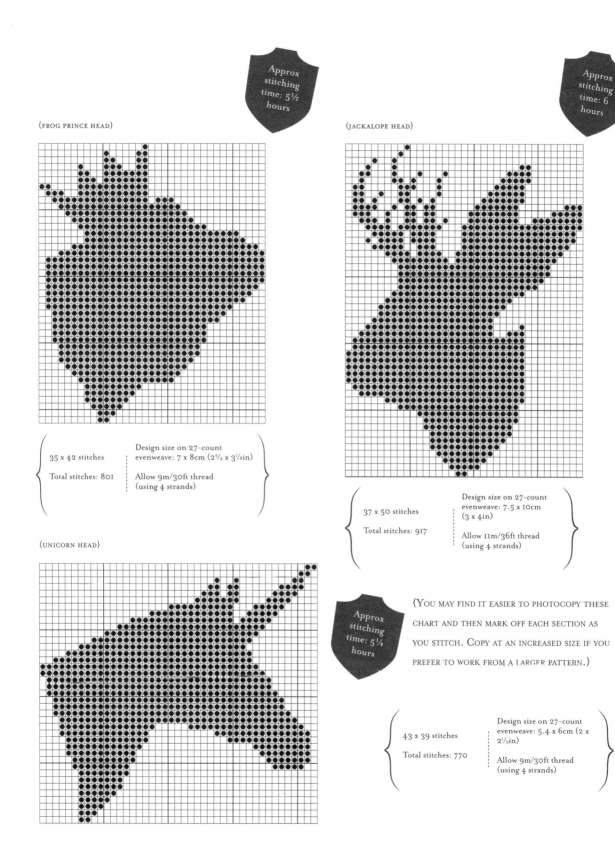

{FROG PRINCE HEAD}

Approx stitching time: 5½ hours

35 x 42 stitches

Total stitches: 801

Design size on 27-count evenweave: 7 x 8cm (2³⁄₄ x 3¹⁄₈in)

Allow 9m/30ft thread (using 4 strands)

{JACKALOPE HEAD}

Approx stitching time: 6 hours

37 x 50 stitches

Total stitches: 917

Design size on 27-count evenweave: 7.5 x 10cm (3 x 4in)

Allow 11m/36ft thread (using 4 strands)

{UNICORN HEAD}

Approx stitching time: 5¼ hours

43 x 39 stitches

Total stitches: 770

Design size on 27-count evenweave: 5.4 x 6cm (2 x 2¹⁄₃in)

Allow 9m/30ft thread (using 4 strands)

{YOU MAY FIND IT EASIER TO PHOTOCOPY THESE CHART AND THEN MARK OFF EACH SECTION AS YOU STITCH. COPY AT AN INCREASED SIZE IF YOU PREFER TO WORK FROM A LARGER PATTERN.}

Enchanted Forest Miniatures

117

The Crown

NLIKE MODERN KINGS AND QUEENS, who only wear their crowns on very special occasions, the rulers of Storyland keep them permanently attached to their heads. Well, obviously not literally, but they would never be seen in public without their crowns – it is a mark of their power and importance and all-round general greatness. They wouldn't want to miss out on an opportunity to remind everybody of that. Besides, I think that if I had a crown I would wear it all the time simply because it would look incredibly awesome.

However, there is a downside: crowns are really quite heavy, which means that if you wear one all the time you are eventually bound to end up with a bit of a dented head (and a constant headache). Most Storyland kings and queens are prepared to put up with this because nobody ever sees them without their crown, but occasionally a royal will be displaced before they die and it can be highly embarrassing for them to spend the rest of their days walking around with an oddly shaped head as a constant reminder of all that they have lost.

With reference to this, I don't really know why some sort of lightweight crown has not made its way into fashion.

Maybe I have found a gap in the market?

Stargazer Tote

{SUPPLIES}

27-count ivory evenweave fabric, 42 x 82cm (16½ x 32in) – 28-count fabric would also work for this design

Stranded cotton embroidery thread in Black (Anchor No. 403/DMC No. 310) and metallic gold embroidery thread (Kreinik Fine Braid #8, 002 Gold)

Tapestry needle, size 24 or 26

Small, sharp scissors

Cream cotton backing fabric, approximately 42 x 82cm (16½ x 32in)

Sewing machine or needle and cream sewing thread

Fabric scissors or pinking shears

Thick cotton tape for straps, 160cm (63in)

{IF YOU WANT THE BAG TO BE WASHABLE, WASH ALL FABRIC BEFORE CUTTING TO SIZE AND MAKING UP.}

1.
Cut a piece of evenweave fabric to 42 x 82cm (16½ x 32in) – if you are using a roller frame or wish to add a little margin for error, then cut the fabric slightly larger to begin with and then you can trim it down to this size when you have finished stitching.

2.
Follow the instructions on page 14 to prepare your evenweave fabric. To find the point to start stitching, fold the length of evenweave fabric in half along the longest edge and then fold one of the sides back on itself to meet the first fold, pressing the middle of the fold with your fingers to mark it. Open the latter fold so that you are once again looking at the fabric folded in half, then fold in the other direction (i.e. into quarters), again pressing the centre point to mark it. Mark the centre point where the folds join with your needle or a pin. A large roller frame (with rollers wider than 42cm/16½in) is particularly helpful for this project because there is a lot of fabric, but it is not essential.

3.
Prepare a length of thread as shown on page 15 – the black cotton is stitched with three strands; if you are using Kreinik Fine Braid #8 for the gold stars, you will need to stitch them using a single strand.

4.
Working from the centre point outwards, follow the pattern on pages 130–131 to stitch the star design.

5.
When you have finished stitching, carefully handwash the fabric if necessary and iron it face down over a towel; this will act as a cushion to protect your stitches.

6.
Cut a 42 x 82cm (16½ x 32in) piece of cotton lining fabric and cut the cotton tape to make two 80cm (31½in) straps. The lining fabric must be exactly the same size as the embroidered evenweave when they are laid flat together.

7.

Place the two pieces of fabric together, right sides facing in, and arrange the two straps in between them at either end. Make sure that the straps are not twisted.

8.

Pin all around the edges of the fabric and then sew a 1cm (⅜in) seam along each of the edges with the handles. Sew only the short sides together at this point – do not join the two long edges. Secure the loose threads with a couple of backstitches and cut off the excess.

9.

Remove the rest of the pins and press the seams open at each end. Turn the two pieces of fabric the right way out so that you can see your embroidery on one side, the lining on the back and a handle at each end.

10.

Press the two handle ends flat, and then topstitch along each of them just a few millimetres from the edge. This will help to hold the fabric and handles in place and will also make your bag stronger and neater. Again, secure the loose threads by backstitching and trimming the excess.

STEP 8

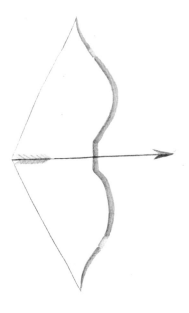

11.

Fold the layers of fabric in half, so that your embroidery is facing outwards and the handles are together at the top, and then pin along the two sides. Sew a 1cm (⅜in) seam along each side (see below). Snip off the four corners, taking care not to cut into the seams.

12.

Press the seams open and trim the excess fabric so that you are left with only a few millimetres on either side of the seam. Then turn the bag inside out and press each seam flat.

13.

You now need to sew another seam along each of the edges that you have just pressed flat. This second seam – about 1cm/⅜in wide – will hide all of the raw edges on the inside of your bag and will also make it much stronger (see right). Secure the end of the thread with a couple of backstitches, and then weave it in between the two layers of fabric, pull the needle and thread out of the back and cut off the excess. You should now be left with a magnificently sturdy tote bag that you can use to carry all manner of heavy items.

STEP 13

STEP 11

{STARGAZER}

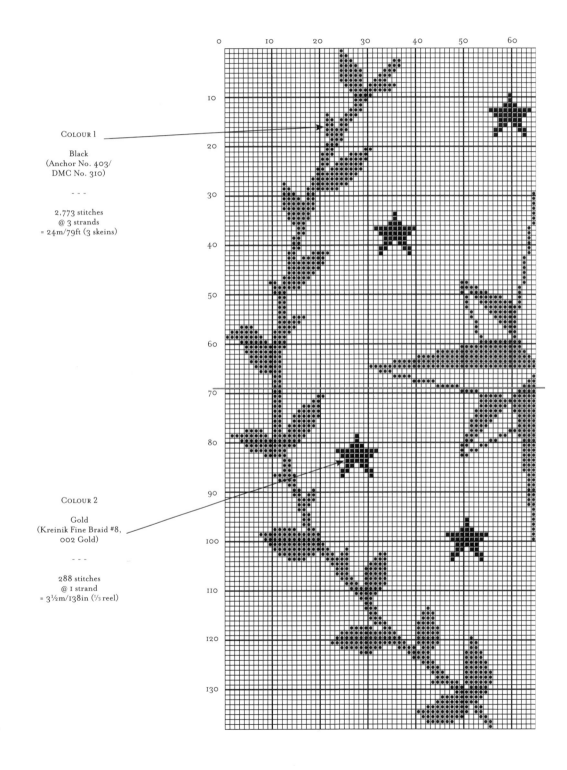

Colour 1

Black
(Anchor No. 403/
DMC No. 310)

- - -

2,773 stitches
@ 3 strands
= 24m/79ft (3 skeins)

Colour 2

Gold
(Kreinik Fine Braid #8,
002 Gold)

- - -

288 stitches
@ 1 strand
= 3½m/138in (⅓ reel)

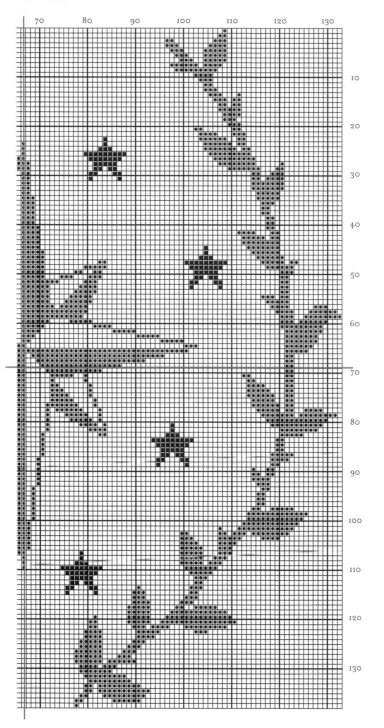

133 x 138 stitches

Total stitches: 3,061

Design size on 27-count
evenweave: 25 x 26cm
(10 x 10¼in)

{YOU MAY FIND IT EASIER TO
PHOTOCOPY THIS CHART, STICK
THE SEPARATE SECTIONS TOGETHER
AND THEN MARK OFF EACH SECTION
AS YOU STITCH. COPY AT AN
INCREASED SIZE IF YOU PREFER TO
WORK FROM A LARGER PATTERN.}

Stargazer Tote

So Long, Farewell

I HAVE BUT SCRATCHED THE SURFACE of all there is to see here in Storyland; however, it is probably time we were on our way. I have found the residents of Storyland to be most generous hosts, but it is always better not to outstay your welcome. Mr Fox has his next scheme to plot, and although he is too polite to say so, he can't exactly do it with me tagging along.

I dare say you have things you should be getting back to as well, so dig out your key, say your goodbyes and scurry back through the towering trees to that crooked old doorframe from whence you came.

It has been a pleasure – you are welcome back any time.

Until then... Toodle pip!

Storyland Sampler

{SUPPLIES}

32-count taupe-coloured linen, 22 x 50cm (8¾ x 20in)

Stranded cotton embroidery thread in Dark Purple (Anchor No. 873/DMC No. 3740), Mid-Purple (Anchor No. 871/DMC No. 3041), Cream (Anchor No. 926/DMC No. 712) and Pale Taupe (Anchor No. 232/ DMC No. 452)

Tapestry needle, size 26 or 28

Small, sharp scissors

Cream cotton backing fabric, approximately 22 x 50cm (8¾ x 20in)

Sewing machine or needle and taupe sewing thread (to match linen)

Fabric scissors or pinking shears

20cm (8in) wooden bell pull ends

Thin taupe-coloured ribbon, approximately 80cm (31½in)

1.
Cut a piece of linen to 22 x 50cm (8¾ x 20in) – if you wish to add a little margin for error, then cut the fabric slightly larger to begin with and then you can trim it down to this size when you have finished stitching.

2.
Follow the instructions on pages 14–15 to prepare your fabric, find its centre point and prepare a length of thread – the design is stitched using two strands. You can use a hoop or roller frame to hold the fabric while you stitch if you find it helpful, but this is not essential.

3.
Working from the centre point outwards, follow the pattern on pages 136–137 to stitch the sampler. (Follow the instructions on page 16 to start stitching.)

4.
When you have finished stitching, carefully handwash the fabric, if necessary, and iron it face down over a towel; this will act as a cushion to protect your stitches.

5.
Cut a 22 x 50cm (8¾ x 20in) piece of cotton lining fabric – the lining fabric must be exactly the same size as the embroidered linen when they are laid flat together. Place the two pieces of fabric together, right sides in, and pin around the edge. Sew a 1cm (⅜in) seam along each of the long edges. Only sew each of the long sides together at this point – do not join the two short edges. Secure the loose threads with a couple of backstitches and cut off the excess.

STEP 5

6.

Press the seams open, and then turn the two pieces of fabric the right way out, so that you can see your embroidery on one side and the lining on the back.

7.

Lay the embroidered linen face down over a towel and iron on the back to ensure all creases have been removed and the seams pressed flat. Then topstitch along each of the long edges just a few millimetres from the edge. This will help to hold the fabric in place and will also make your sampler look flatter and neater. Again secure the loose threads by backstitching and trimming the excess.

STEP 8

8.

Fold the open top edge back on itself by about 5cm (2in) and pin in place. Repeat for the bottom edge and sew a line along each, roughly 1–2cm (³⁄₈–¾in) above the raw edge on the back – you will see a seam on the front about 3–4cm (1¼–1½in) deep (see below left). These deep seams form the pair of channels that will hold your bell pull ends.

9.

Once you have sewn the seams, you may wish to remove a few threads from the raw edges or trim them with pinking shears to prevent them from fraying further. Remove one of the finials from the bottom bell pull end, pass the rod through the channel you have just sewn, and then replace the finial (see below).

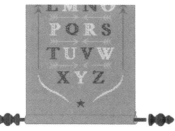

STEP 9

10.

Cut two pieces of ribbon to approximately 40cm (15¾in) each. Remove one of the finials from the top bell pull end, wrap the end of a ribbon around it and replace the finial so that it holds the ribbon in place. Remove the second finial, pass the rod through the channel at the top of your embroidery and then wind the end of the second piece of ribbon around it before replacing the finial. Tie the ribbons together and hang (see below).

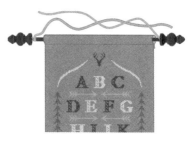

STEP 10

{WHY NOT USE SOME OF THE LETTERS FROM THIS ALPHABET PATTERN TO PERSONALISE YOUR PROJECTS BY STITCHING YOUR INITIALS ONTO THEM?}

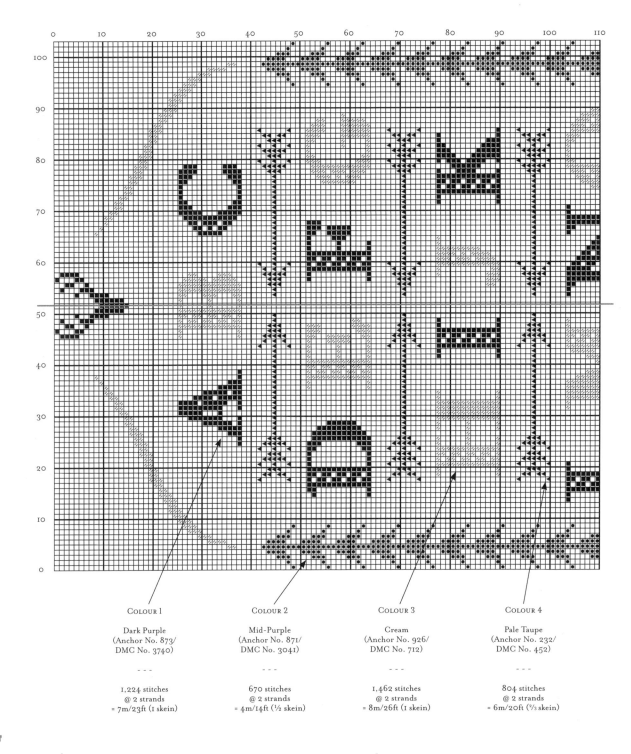

COLOUR 1

Dark Purple
(Anchor No. 873/
DMC No. 3740)

- - -

1,224 stitches
@ 2 strands
= 7m/23ft (1 skein)

COLOUR 2

Mid-Purple
(Anchor No. 871/
DMC No. 3041)

- - -

670 stitches
@ 2 strands
= 4m/14ft (½ skein)

COLOUR 3

Cream
(Anchor No. 926/
DMC No. 712)

- - -

1,462 stitches
@ 2 strands
= 8m/26ft (1 skein)

COLOUR 4

Pale Taupe
(Anchor No. 232/
DMC No. 452)

- - -

804 stitches
@ 2 strands
= 6m/20ft (⅔ skein)

{STORYLAND SAMPLER PATTERN}

Approx stitching time: 28 hours

Centre Points

103 x 220 stitches

Total stitches: 4,160

Design size on 32-count linen:
16.5 x 35cm (6½ x 13¾in)

{YOU MAY FIND IT EASIER TO PHOTOCOPY THIS CHART, STICK THE SEPARATE SECTIONS TOGETHER AND THEN MARK OFF EACH SECTION AS YOU STITCH. COPY AT AN INCREASED SIZE IF YOU PREFER TO WORK FROM A LARGER PATTERN.}

Suppliers

WHAT DELILAH DID
Modern cross stitch patterns, kits, supplies and accessories.
www.whatdelilahdid.com

{SEW AND SO}
Massive range of cross stitch fabrics, threads, kits and accessories
www.sewandso.co.uk

{SIESTA FRAMES}
Embroidery hoops, frames and accessories
www.siestaframes.com

{WOOL FELT COMPANY}
100% wool felt, good quality and lovely colours
www.woolfeltcompany.co.uk

{HOBBYCRAFT}
Assorted craft supplies – button blanks, glue, scissors, etc.
www.hobbycraft.co.uk

{THE FEATHER COMPANY}
Well-made feather cushion pads, all shapes and sizes
www.thefeathercompany.com

{THE FENT SHOP}
Wide range of fabrics, trimmings and accessories – good value
www.thefentshopkingslynn.co.uk

{QUALITY NEEDLECRAFT}
Cross stitch kits and accessories – excellent, friendly service
www.qualityneedlecraft.co.uk

{CLOTH HOUSE}
Outstanding range of fabrics and trimmings
www.clothhouse.com

{DMR FRAMING}
Picture frames, all styles with or without glass – really helpful
www.dmrframing.co.uk

{LIBERTY}
Beautiful haberdashery, lots of kits and trimmings
www.liberty.co.uk

{JOHN JAMES NEEDLES}
Great range of embroidery needles, including easy-threading versions.
www.jjneedles.com

{ORGANIC TEXTILE COMPANY}
Brilliant selection of organic and fair trade cotton fabrics.
Especially good for plain backing fabrics.
www.organiccotton.biz

About the Author

Sophie Simpson (aka Delilah) is the creator behind embroidery business, What Delilah Did. She runs a successful blog and online shop where she sells her distinctive embroidery patterns and kits to customers all over the world.

Her inaugural collection was launched by prestigious London department store, Liberty, and her kits are sold in boutique haberdasheries and lifestyle shops throughout the United Kingdom.

When she is not dreaming up things for her own business, Sophie works as a freelance designer, with regular projects featured in British magazine CrossSticher and a number of other publications, most recently Pearl Lowe's Vintage Home and Mollie Makes Woodland Friends. Her designs, which are an amalgamation of antique heirloom embroidery and modern design, are attracting a whole new generation to this age-old craft.

A mildly eccentric girl with a rather overactive imagination, Sophie lives in a sleepy market town in Norfolk, England and loves folk music, baking, period dramas, whales and all things handmade. You can follow her crafty adventures on her blog at www.whatdelilahdid.com.

Acknowledgements

I must admit I am not the world's biggest fan of endless thank you lists – not because I am not thankful of course, but simply because having been brought up by a lady who is (quite rightly) formidably strict when it comes to good manners, I generally prefer to thank people personally as I go along. That said however, there are three particular notes of formal thanks that this book would be incomplete without:

Firstly to Mum and Dave, without whose endless support and encouragement I could never have finished this book. Through tantrums, computer breakdowns and assorted minor and major catastrophes you have kept me going with help, advice and on occasion even meals on wheels! May every young(ish) person brave/ mad enough to set up their own business be lucky enough to have parents as awesome as you to back them up.

Secondly to my editor Amy, for seeking me out and offering me the opportunity to realise a long-held dream; and to everybody at Collins & Brown for taking a chance on me and allowing me the freedom to do exactly what I wanted with this book. I could not have wished for a better introduction to the world of publishing.

And finally, an enormous thank you to all of the wonderful customers and stitchers the world over who have supported my work thus far. You have given me the confidence to get here and none of this would have been possible without you. I will be eternally grateful. Thank you!

First published in the United Kingdom in 2013 by
Collins & Brown
10 Southcombe Street
London
W14 0RA

An imprint of Anova Books Company Ltd

Distributed in the United States and Canada by
Sterling Publishing Co, 387 Park Avenue South,
New York, NY 10016-8810, USA

ISBN 978-1-90844-939-9

A CIP catalogue record for this book is available
from the British Library.

10 9 8 7 6 5 4 3 2 1

Photography by Rachel Whiting
Illustrations by Kuo Kang Chen

Reproduction by Mission, Hong Kong
Printed by 1010 Printing International Ltd, China

This book can be ordered direct from
the publisher at www.anovabooks.com

Whatever the craft, we have the book for you – just head
straight to Collins & Brown crafty HeadQuarters!

LoveCrafts is the one-stop destination for all things crafty,
with the very latest news and information about all our
books and authors. It doesn't stop there…

Enter our fabulous competitions and win great prizes
Download free patterns from our talented authors
Collect LoveCrafts loyalty points and receive
special offers on all our books

Join our crafting community at LoveCrafts –
we look forward to meeting you!